Watercolors by Jodi

ISBN-13: 978-1-4796-1019-8 (Hardback)
Library of Congress Control Number: 2018957222

FOREWORD

As Jodi's husband for the past thirty plus years, I have had the privilege of watching her bloom as an artist. Raised in a family of artists, Jodi apparently saw nothing that really sparked her interest until a friend asked her to do a portrait of a pet cat that had recently died. Jodi took the commission, and working from photographs, managed to present the animal in a way that captured its personality. A second commission followed as a second cat exhausted its nine lives, and again she was able to capture the essence of the second animal. Encouraged by these two efforts, Jodi then enrolled in an internet course in watercolor painting which she completed in the next six months. From that point it was off to the races. No matter what the subject Jodi could capture the essence of things and portray that in watercolors, whether it be a leaf or a bug (or a cat).

—Dean P. Richmond

INTRODUCTION

I like to say that I am a "born again" artist. I used to dabble a bit in watercolors, transparent oils, acrylics, pastels, charcoal, and whatever else I could get my hands on back in the 1970's. My mother and most everyone on her side of the family were artists. I was very actively doing art for about 2 years then didn't paint again for about 45 years. The only "training" I had was in October of 2015 when I signed up for a 6 month's on-line course from Anna Mason. Best money I ever spent. It infected me to no end and got my artistic juices flowing.

I paint from photos getting my references from jig-saw puzzles I used to play on FaceBook (Puzzles For Friends), and on-line photo sharing sites (Photos for Artists and Paint My Photo), plus a few other photographers and some of my own photos. I find most of my inspiration through nature. I have not painted en plein air yet, but maybe in my future.

I use only primary colors when painting, and those are Cobalt Blue, Azo Yellow and Alizarin Crimson from M. Graham. I will use a bit of Chinese White at times, but try to keep that at a bare minimum as I do favor preserving the white of the paper with masking fluid over Chinese White.

—Jodi Sones

Watercolors
by Jodi

Abandoned Dreams

The story of this little steam boat is that Elmer Bach, the builder, shared a dream with his daughter, Alma Lee, to go boating up and down the Yaquina River. Sadly, before he finished building his boat, Alma Lee died, so the boat sat in the water as you see it here, unfinished ever since. The weather here in Oregon has taken a toll on Alma Lee, and there is very little left of it now. At high tide, it is hard to even find it. It is located in the Yaquina River, just outside Toledo, Oregon.

Reference photo by Frank Jones of francyfotos
6 1/4" by 8 1/4" on Arches 140 pound cold press watercolor paper

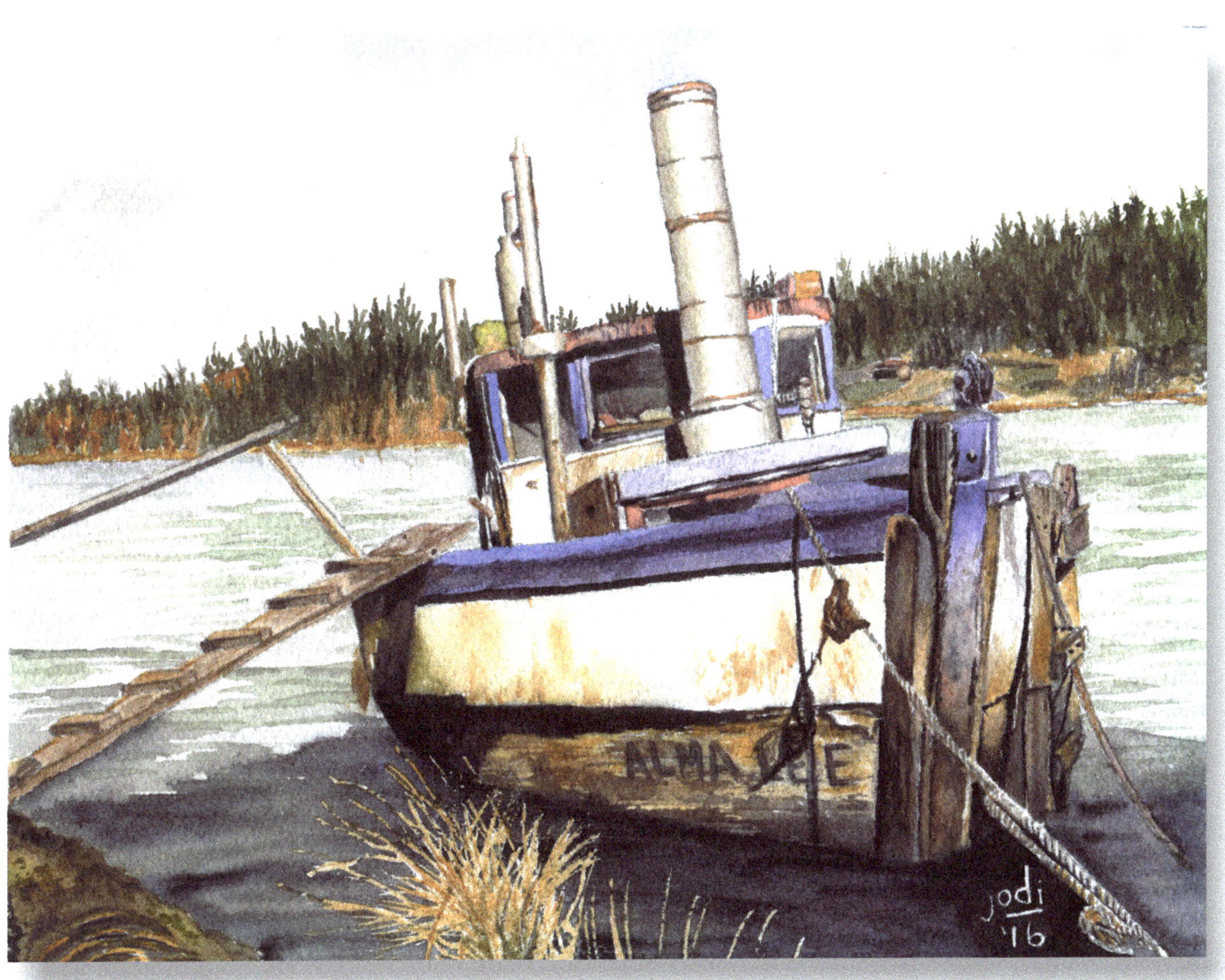
jodi
'16

Forgotten Dreams of Alma Lee

The second of three paintings I did of this little steam boat. The elements don't take long to take over when things are left out for them. It was sad watching this boat slowly disappear.

Reference photo by artist
8 5/4" by 6 ½" on 140 pound Arches cold press watercolor paper

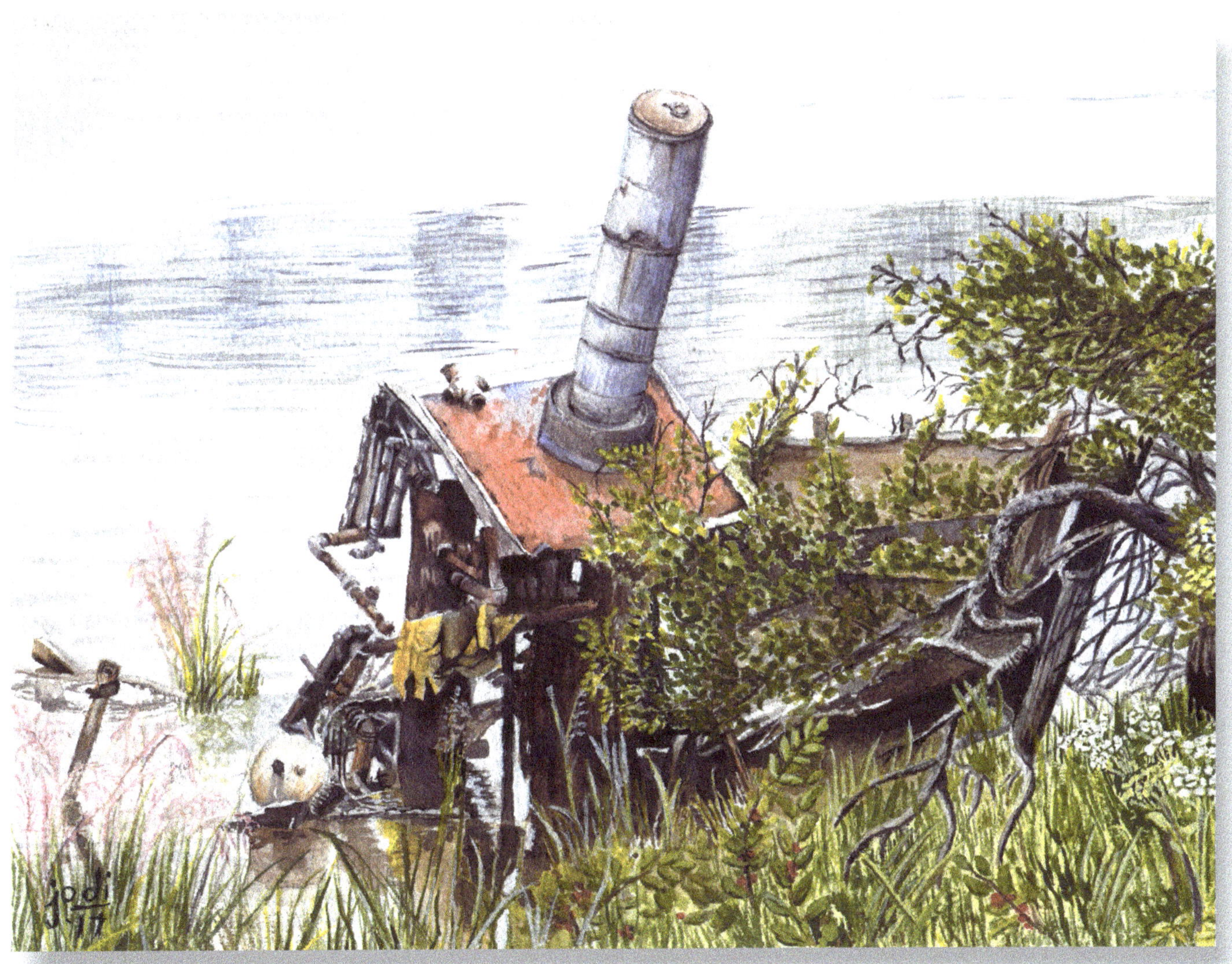

Rest in Peace Sweet Alma Lee

This is the third and last in the life and times of the Alma Lee. This was from my own photo. It was sad when I finished this painting. Almost like I was leaving behind an old friend.

Reference photo by artist
9 3/8" by 6 3/8" on 140 pound Arches cold press watercolor paper

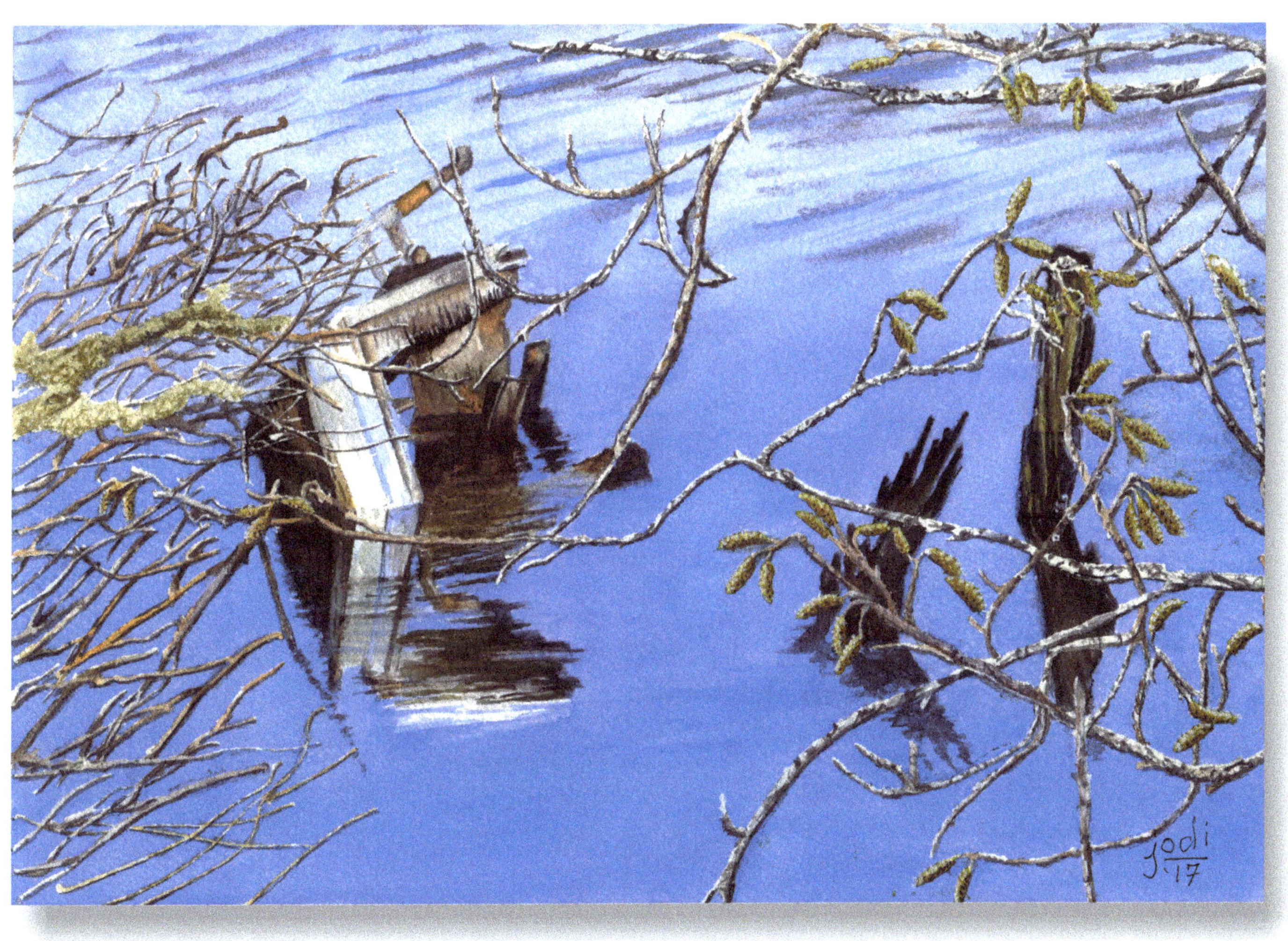
Jodi
'17

My Little Chickadee

I like to make my own Christmas cards every year and this is the painting I used for my 2018 cards. I like these little paintings and love painting birds.

Reference photo by Rodney Campbell
7″ by 6 5/8″ on 140 pound Arches cold press watercolor paper

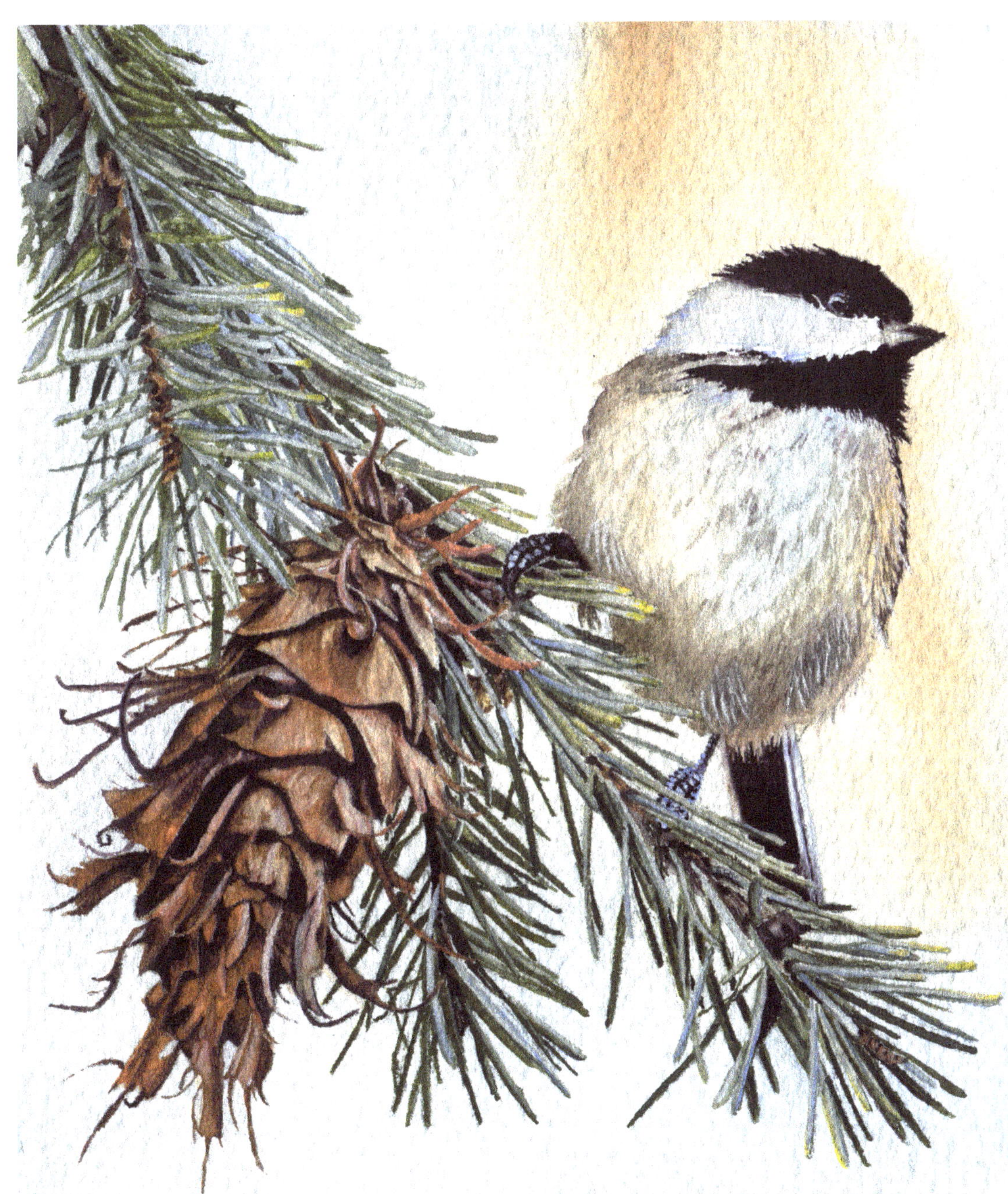
jodi
'18

Yellow Skunks

I love our local indigenous plants here on the central Oregon coast, and this is one of my favorites. It is also known as Swamp Lantern. I understand that this same plant has white bracts east of the Rockies. Its scientific name is Lysichiton americanum. It is one of the first to bloom in early spring. I took this photo myself. They grow in very wet, swampy areas. The more water, the better they like it. Guess that is why they do so well in our area.

Reference photo by artist
7 1/2" by 5 5/8" on Arches 140 pound cold press watercolor paper

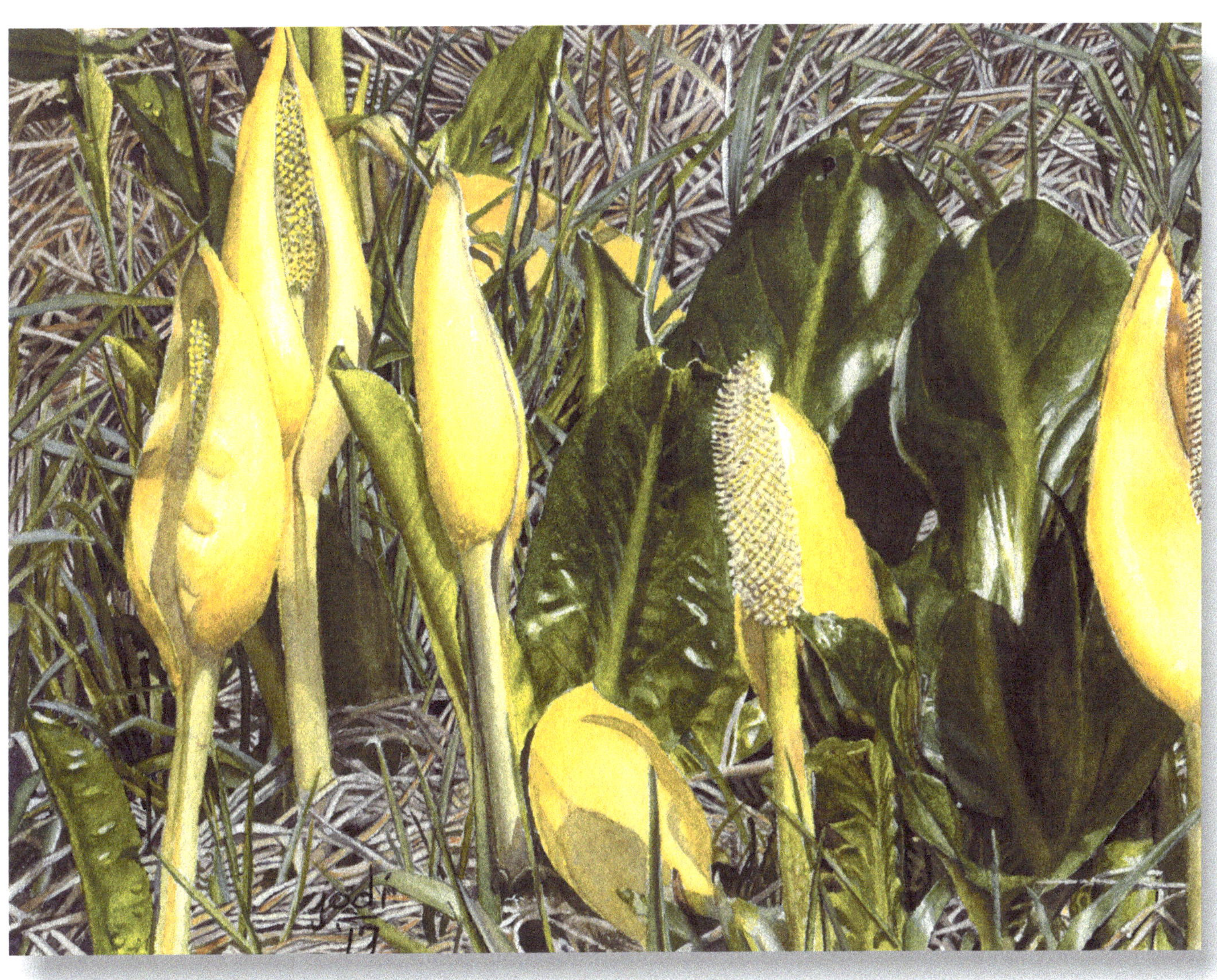

Bubbles

This was fun and quite different for me. It is on black mat-board. I did use Chinese white in all of this as watercolor paints, being mostly transparent except for white, wouldn't have shown up at all.

Inspired by a colored pencil drawing found on Pinterest
12 1/2" by 8 1/2" on black mat-board

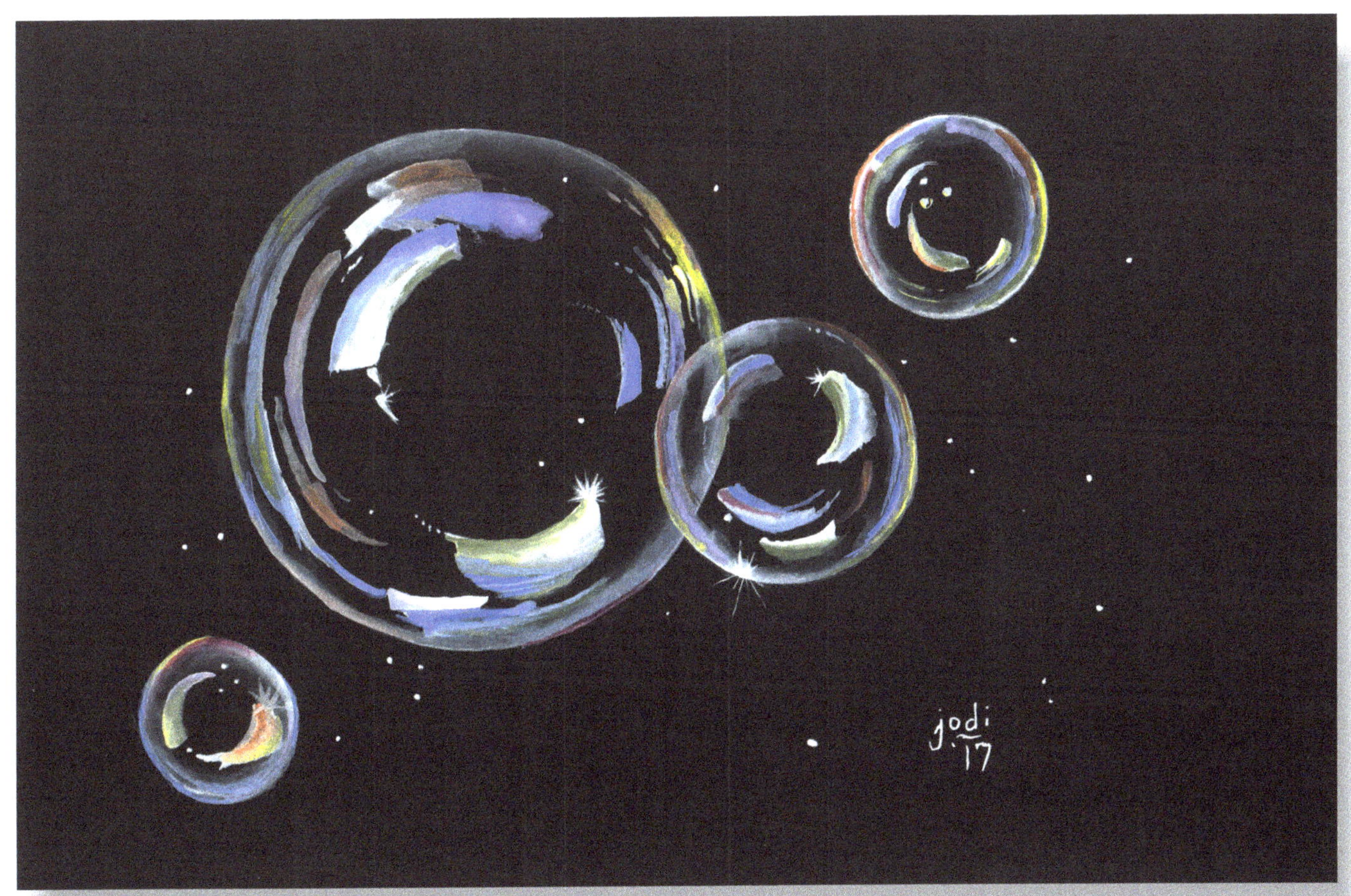
jodi
'17

Autumn Leaves

I love painting leaves and complicated subjects. The colors in this really spoke to me as did the fact that it was all leaves in a kind of collage.

Reference photo is from Puzzles For Friends on FaceBook
6 7/8" by 5" on 140 pound Arches cold press watercolor paper

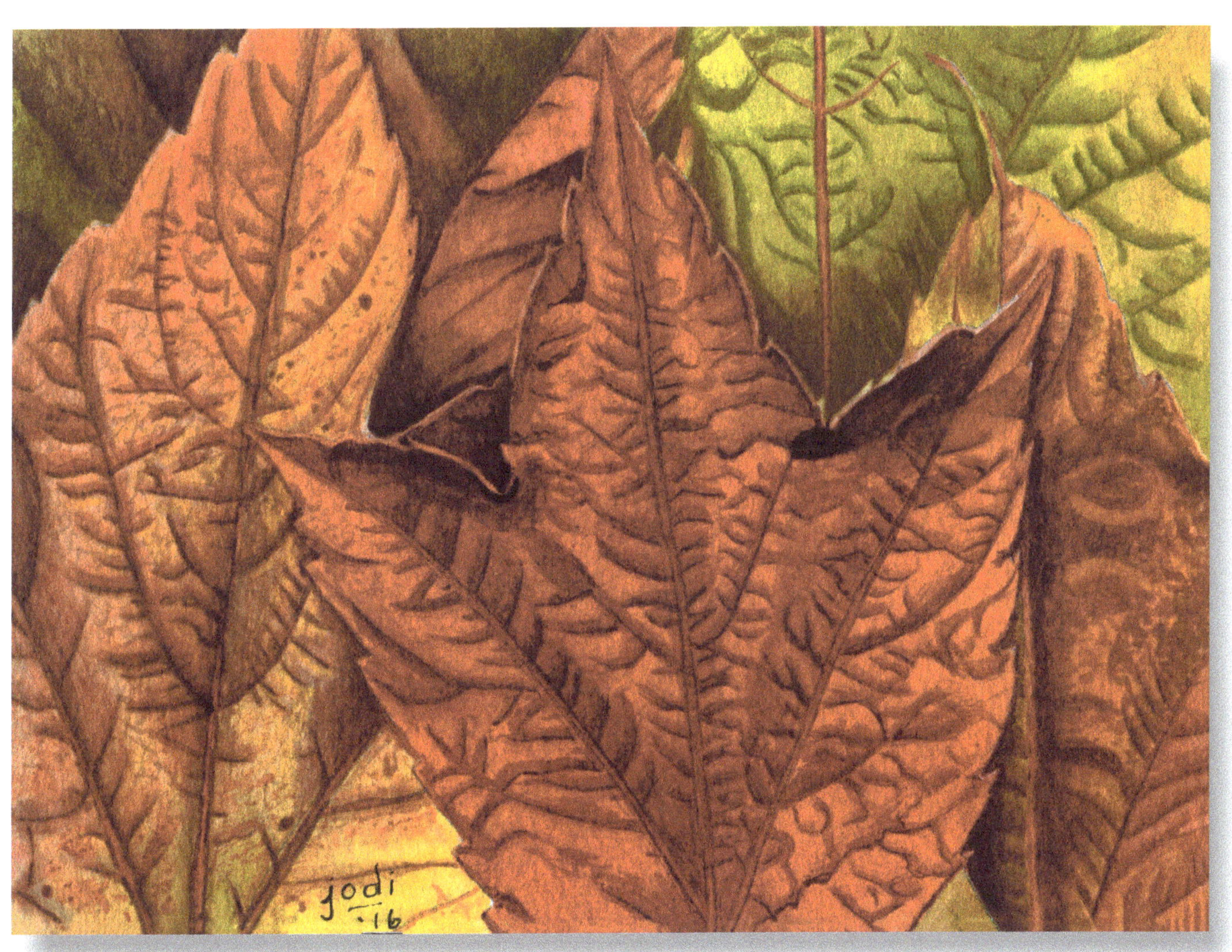
jodi
'16

Large Resting Deer

One of the favorite little, one-or-two-day vacations my husband and I like to take is to Joseph, Oregon, in the upper east corner of Oregon. It is a high mountain area where the Nez Perce once ruled. On one of these trips, we decided to take a drive around the near-by Wallowa Lake. In the back side of the parking lot behind the lake, we spotted this very large deer. At first we drove past it, then I said let me take a photo of it to paint. The rest is history.

Reference photo by artist
9 5/8" by 6" on 140 pound Arches cold press watercolor paper

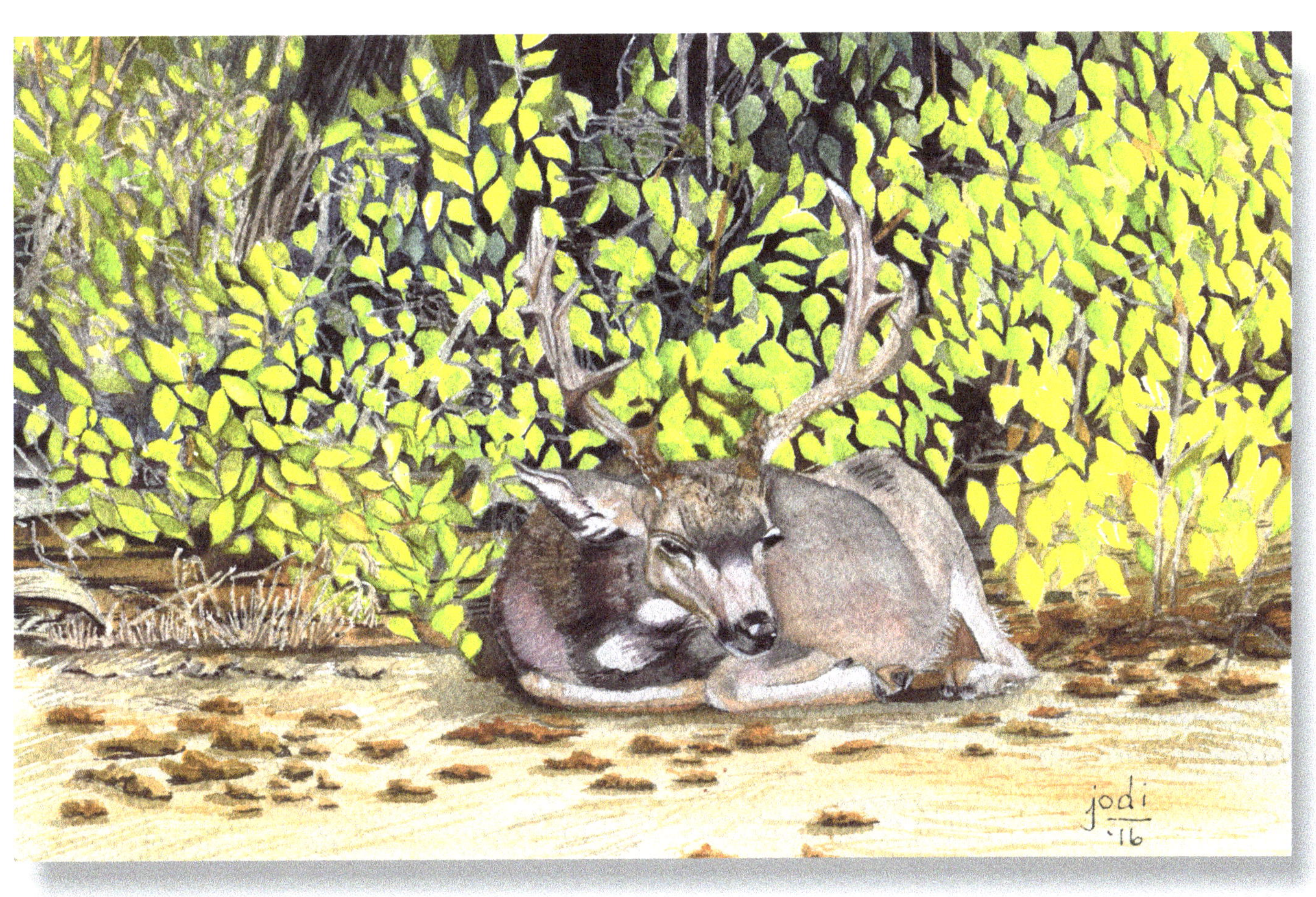
jodi
'16

Ladies on a Poppy Bud

This was a bit of an experiment for me, as are most things I paint. Wanted to see if I could get the "hairs" on the flower bud and stem to look realistic. Don't think I managed that, but do think it turned out cute.

Reference photo from Puzzles For Friends
5 1/4" by 7 1/2" on an old piece of Arches cold press watercolor paper

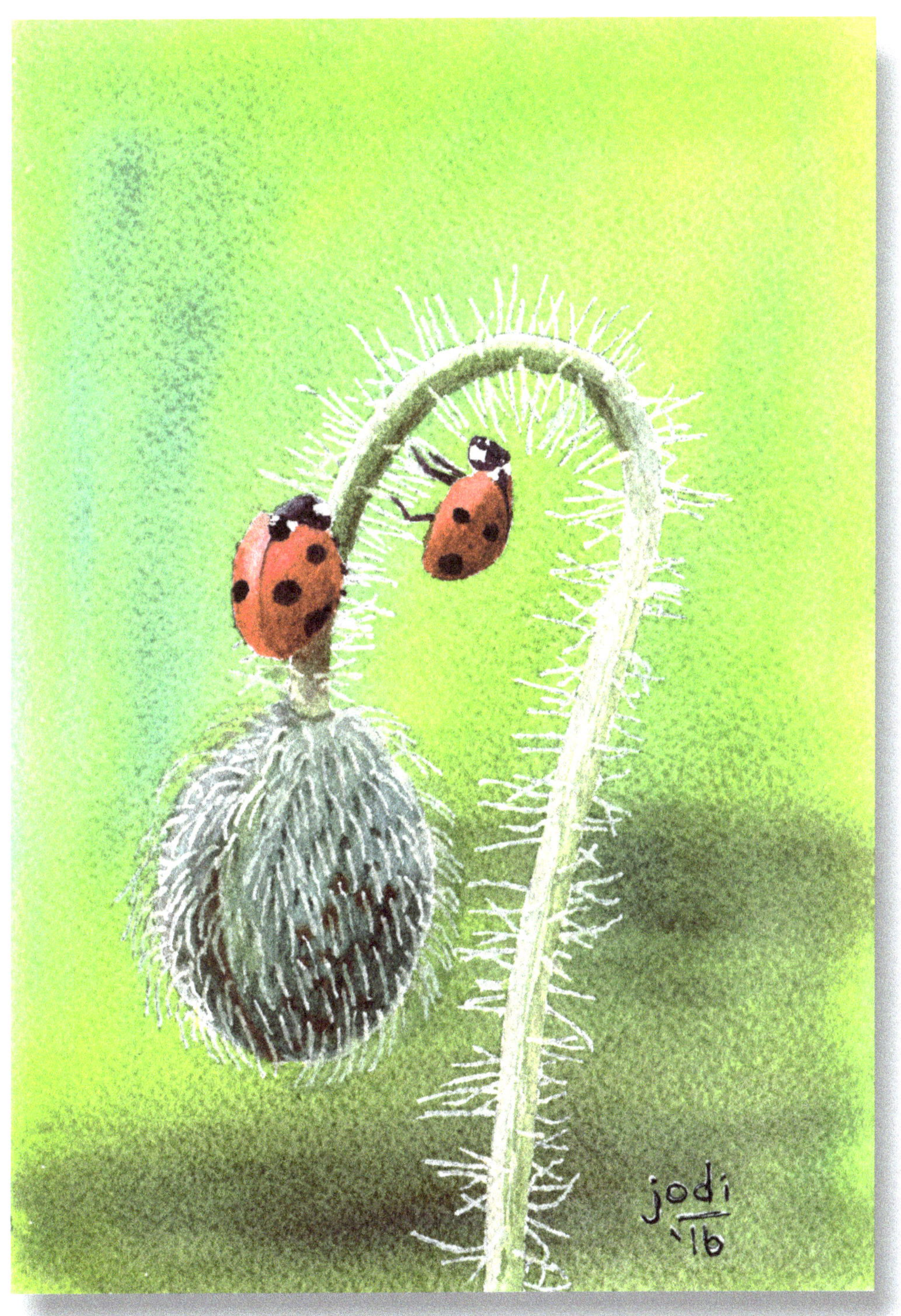
jodi
'16

Pinecones and Needles

One of the most complicated painting I've done. It is from a photo one of my class-mates from high school took. I did use a bit of Chinese White in this painting. It took me about a week to paint, which is quite a long time for a small painting.

Reference photo by Christine Bartlette Truesdale
10" by 14" on Arches 140 pound watercolor paper

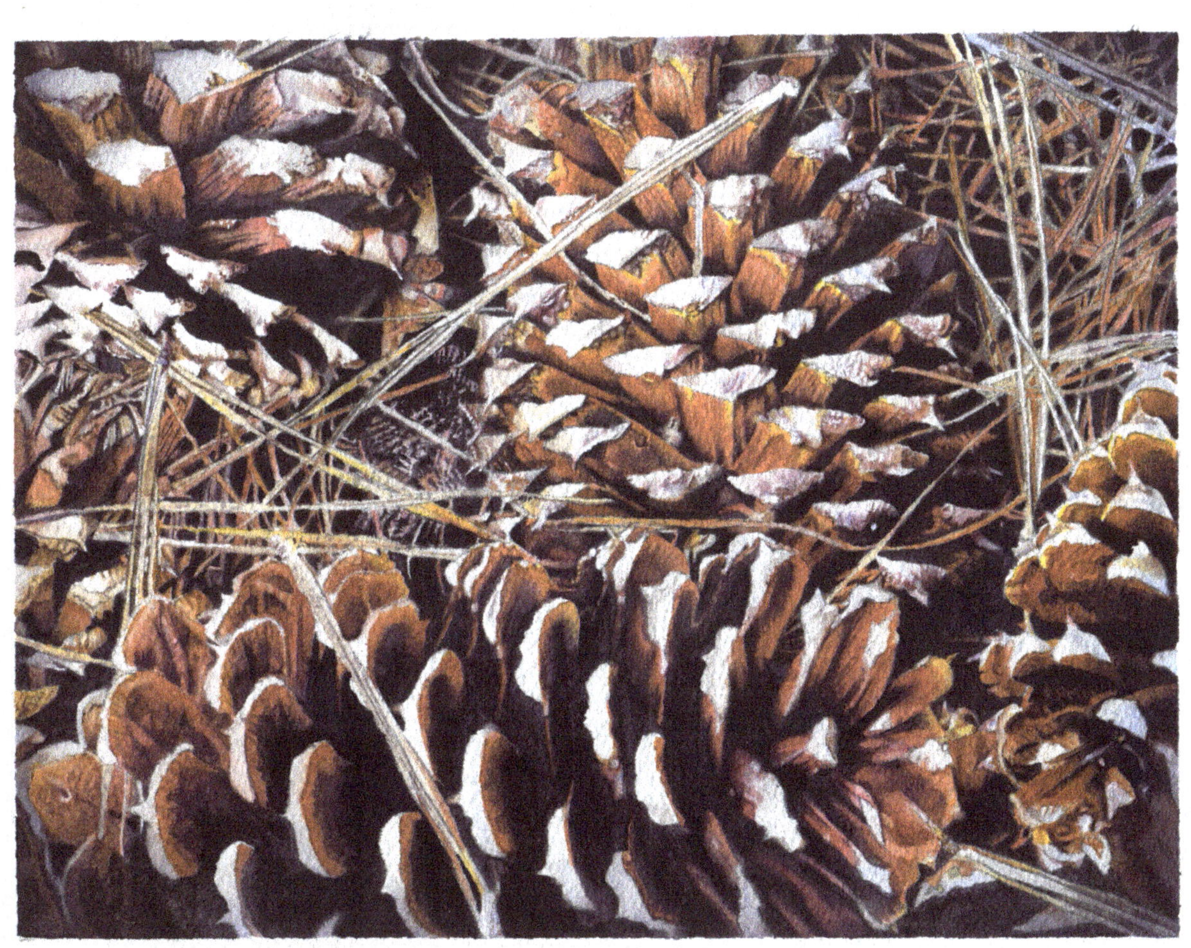
jodi
'16

Creek Street

This was taken on a cruise to Alaska my husband and I took in October of 2016. These buildings were part of the red light district during the gold rush in the late 1800's in Ketchikan. I did this on the back side of mat-board, which was not an easy thing to do. Don't think I will try that again! Anyway, I had to use quite a bit of Chinese white as it was near impossible to preserve the white of the mat-board.

Reference photo by artist
10 3/4" by 7 7/8" on mat-board

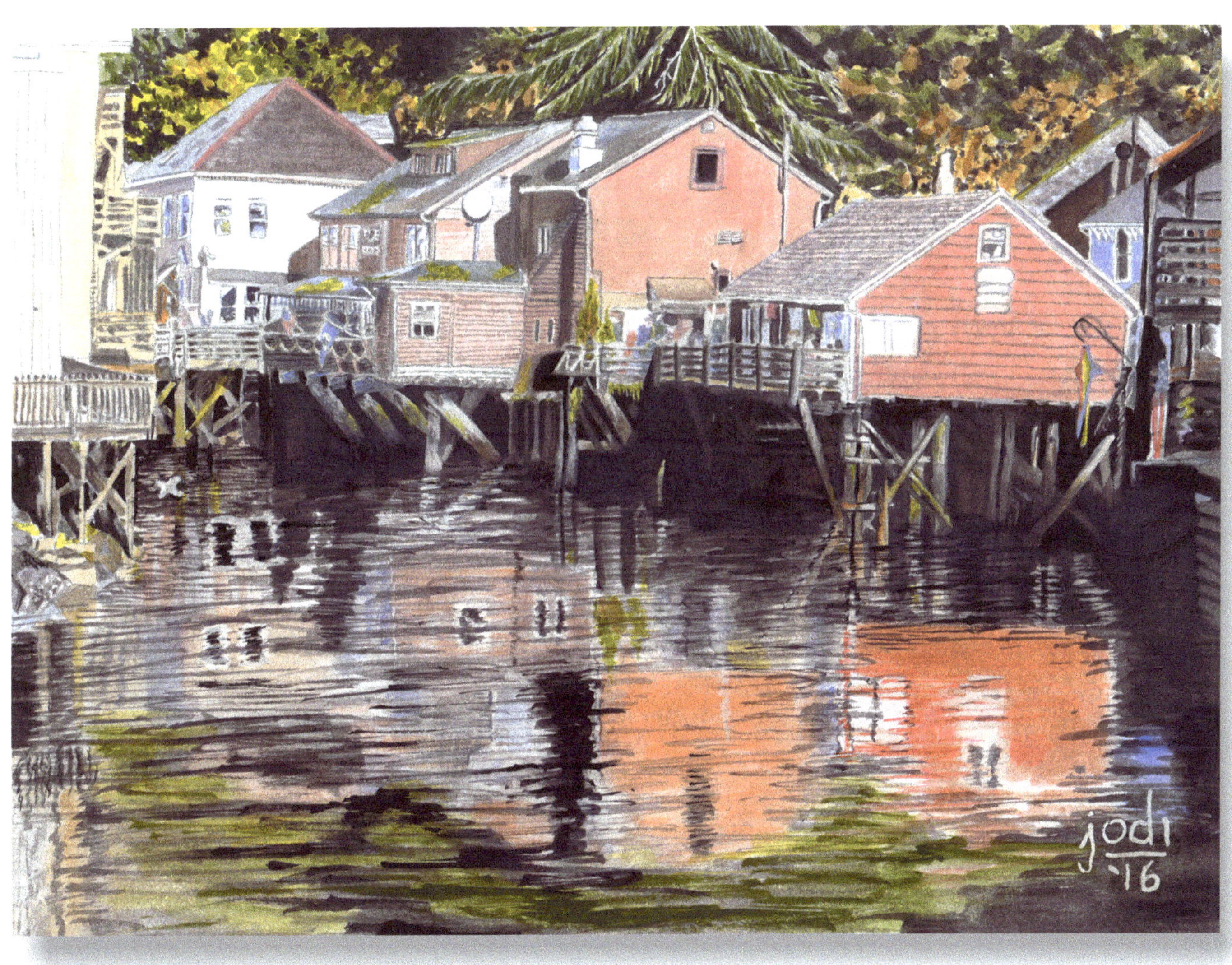
jodi
'16

Pink Rose

The photographer of this beautiful rose is a friend of mine on FaceBook, and when I saw that this was one of his photos, I just had to paint it. Getting the pink just right was a real learning experience for me. Alizerian Crimson isn't all that easy to get to a nice pink.

Reference photo by Russ Cahn posted in Photos For Artists
9 1/4" by 5 1/8" on 140 pound Arches cold press watercolor paper

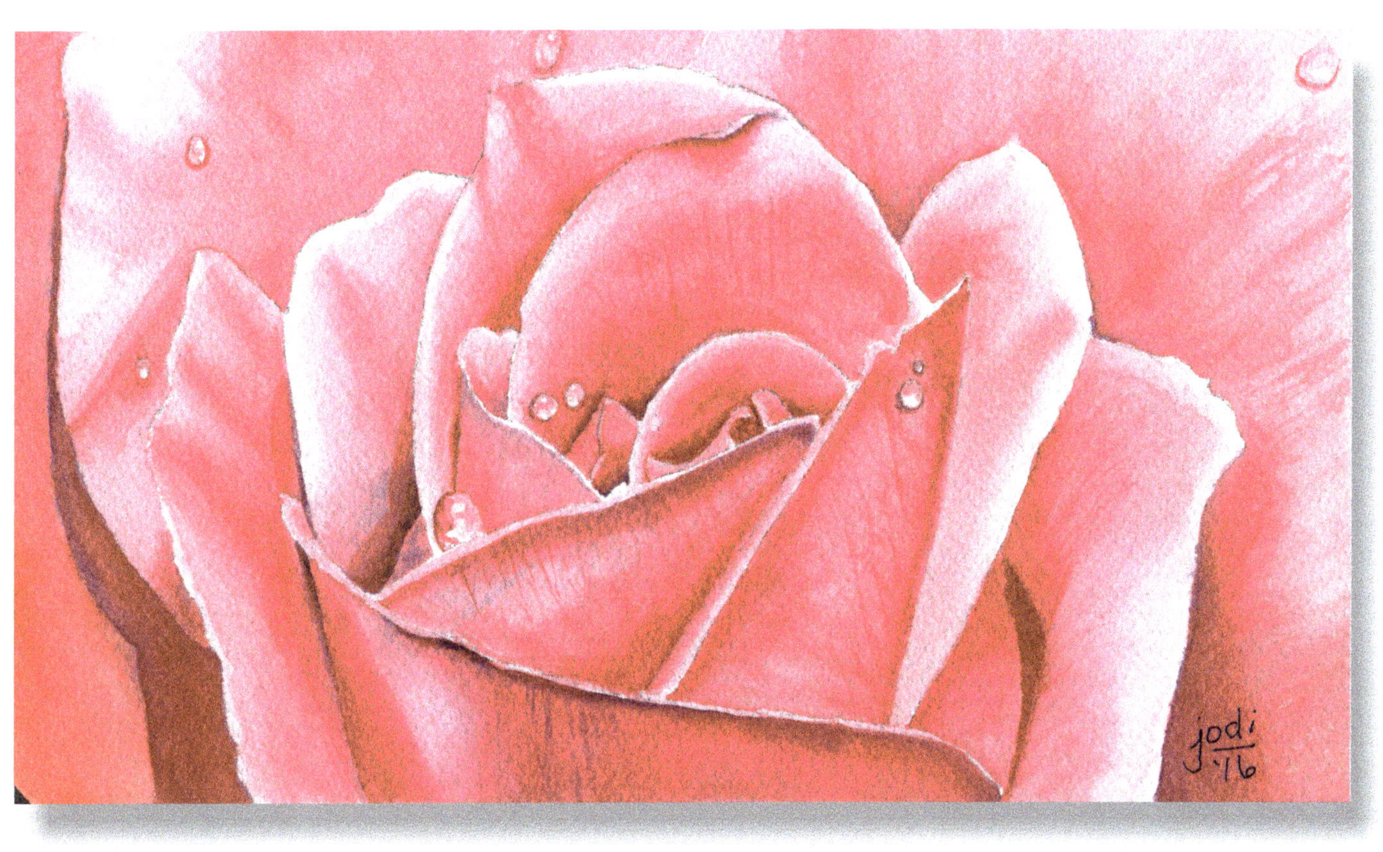
jodi
'16

Pink Cactus Flower

I love the stuff this artist does and couldn't resist this with it's thorns. As usual, this was another learning curve for me, which I love. It is always nice to push your envelope to see how far you can go.

Tutorial by Krzysztof Kowalski
8 1/2" by 10 7/8" on 140 pound Arches cold press watercolor paper

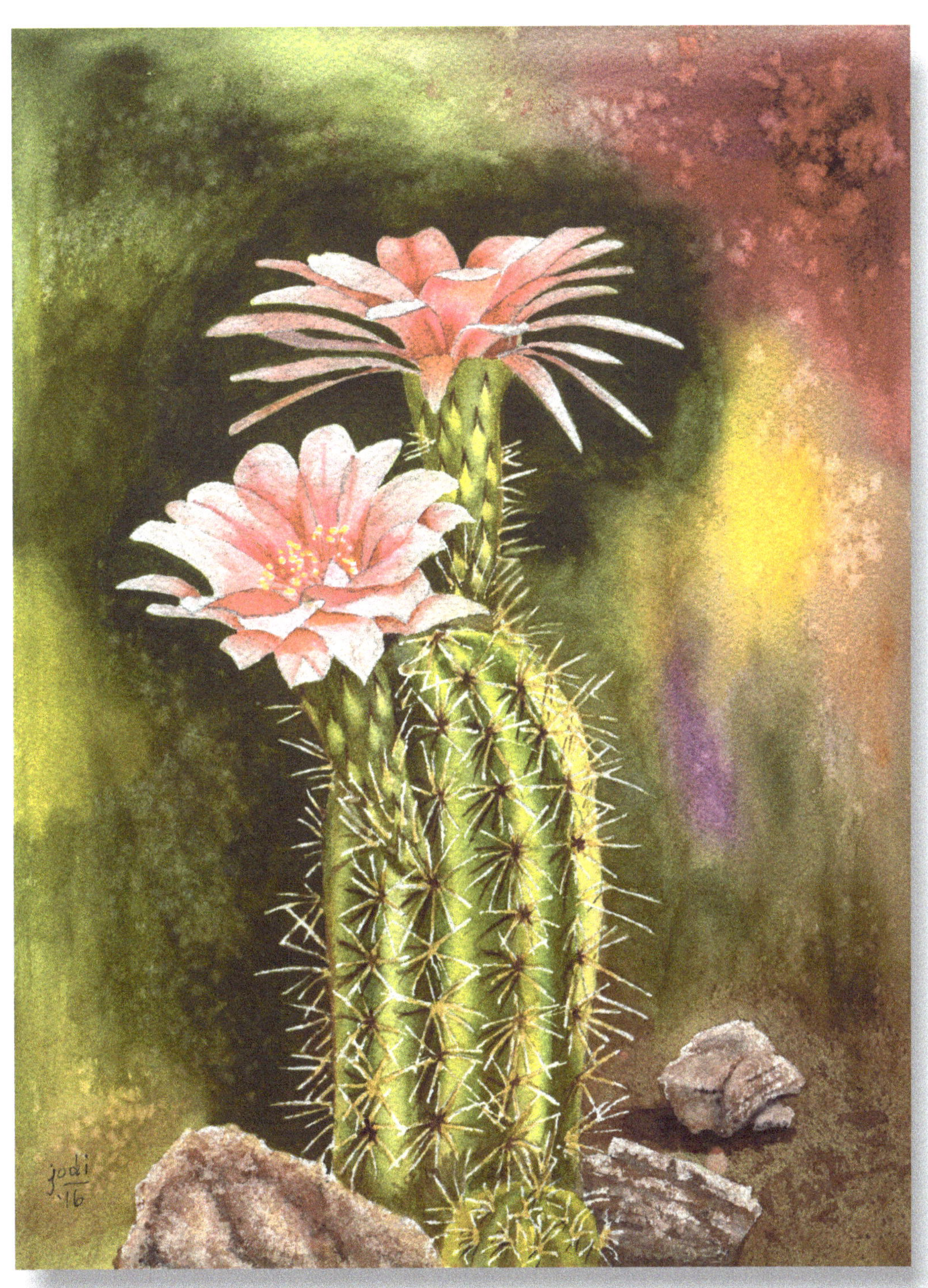
jodi
'16

The White Swan

My first attempt at trying to do water. Pushing that envelope again. Also, the swan was done in a technique called "negative painting" as were the leaves in the background. No white was used in this painting at all.

Reference photo by Russ Bridges in Photos For Artists
6 1/4" by 8 7/8" on 140 pound Arches cold press watercolor paper

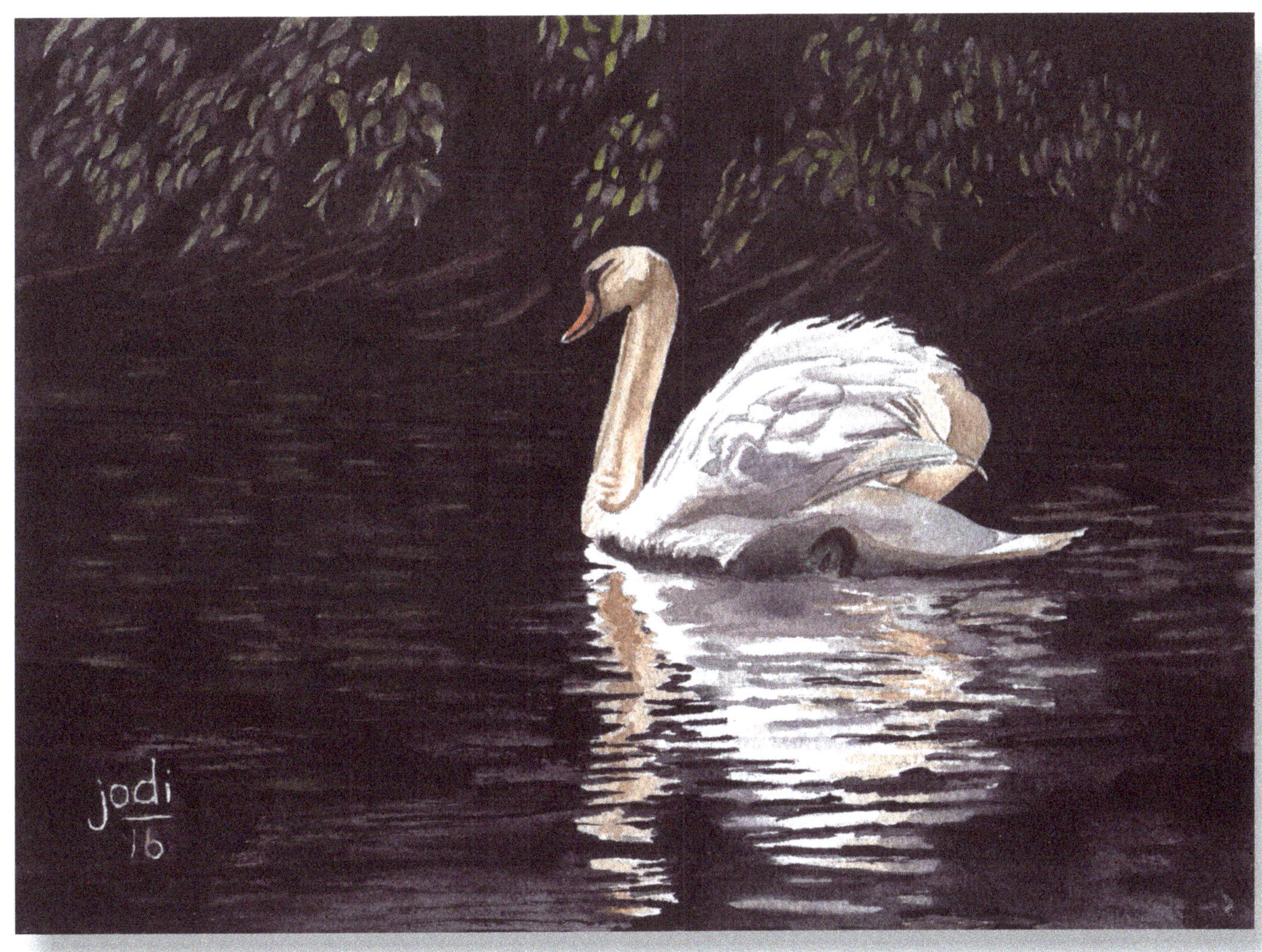
jodi
16

A Little Cottontail Bunny

This is the first time I've tried painting soft fur. Every painting I do seems to be something new to learn for me. Remember, when looking at this, there is no black paint used here nor white. Only the red/blue/yellow primary colors. I mix every color I use to get what I want.

Reference photo by Jodi Newell in Photos For Artists
6" by 9" on Arches cold press watercolor paper

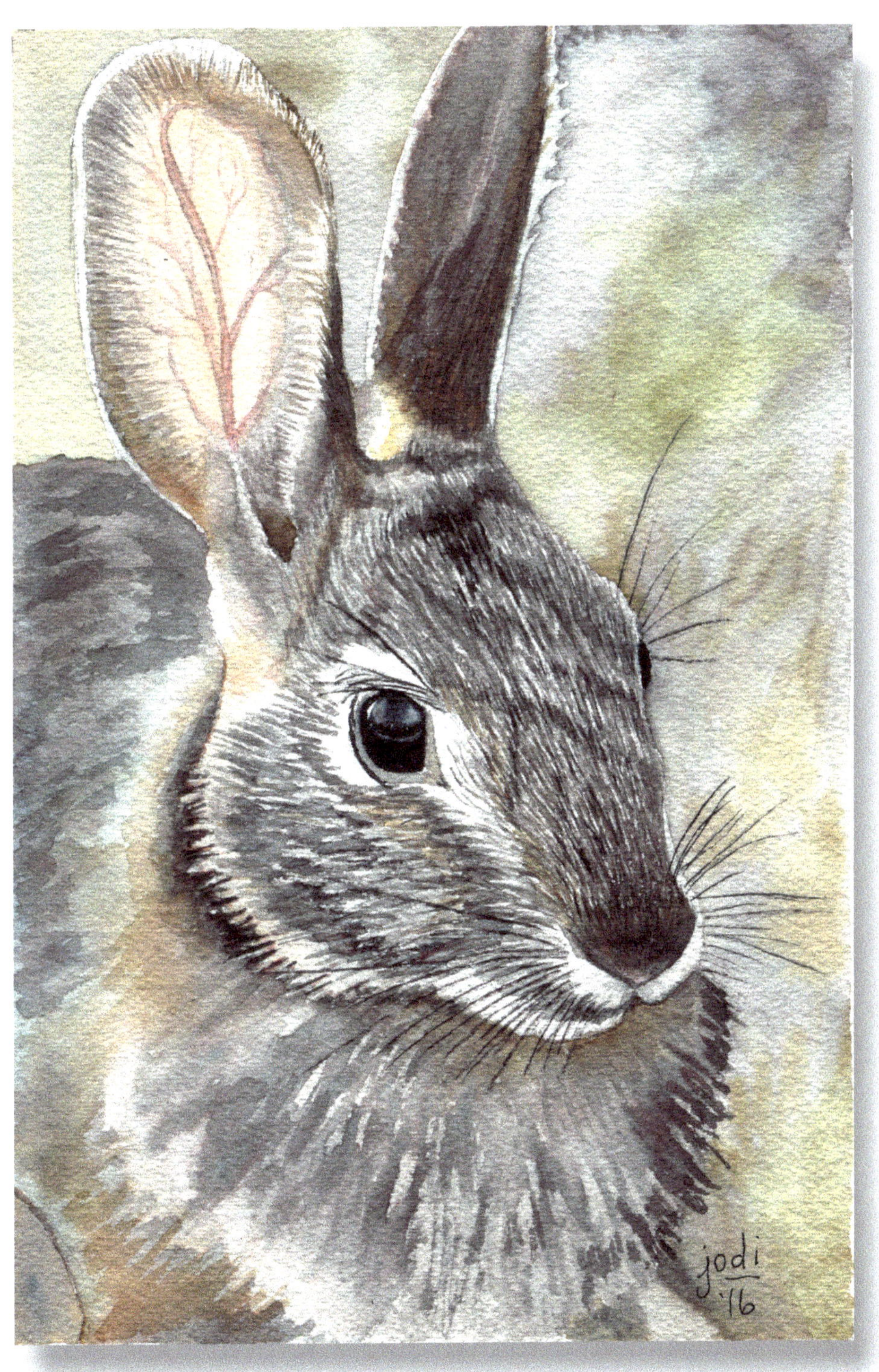
jodi
'16

Beached Posts

Well, I do live on the Oregon coast, so guess I really should do a beach scene or two, right? Again, I haven't painted sand before. Always trying to learn something new with every single thing I paint.

Reference photo submitted by Thomas Zakowski to Puzzles For Friends
5 1/2" by 8 1/4" and is on 140 pound Arches cold press watercolor paper

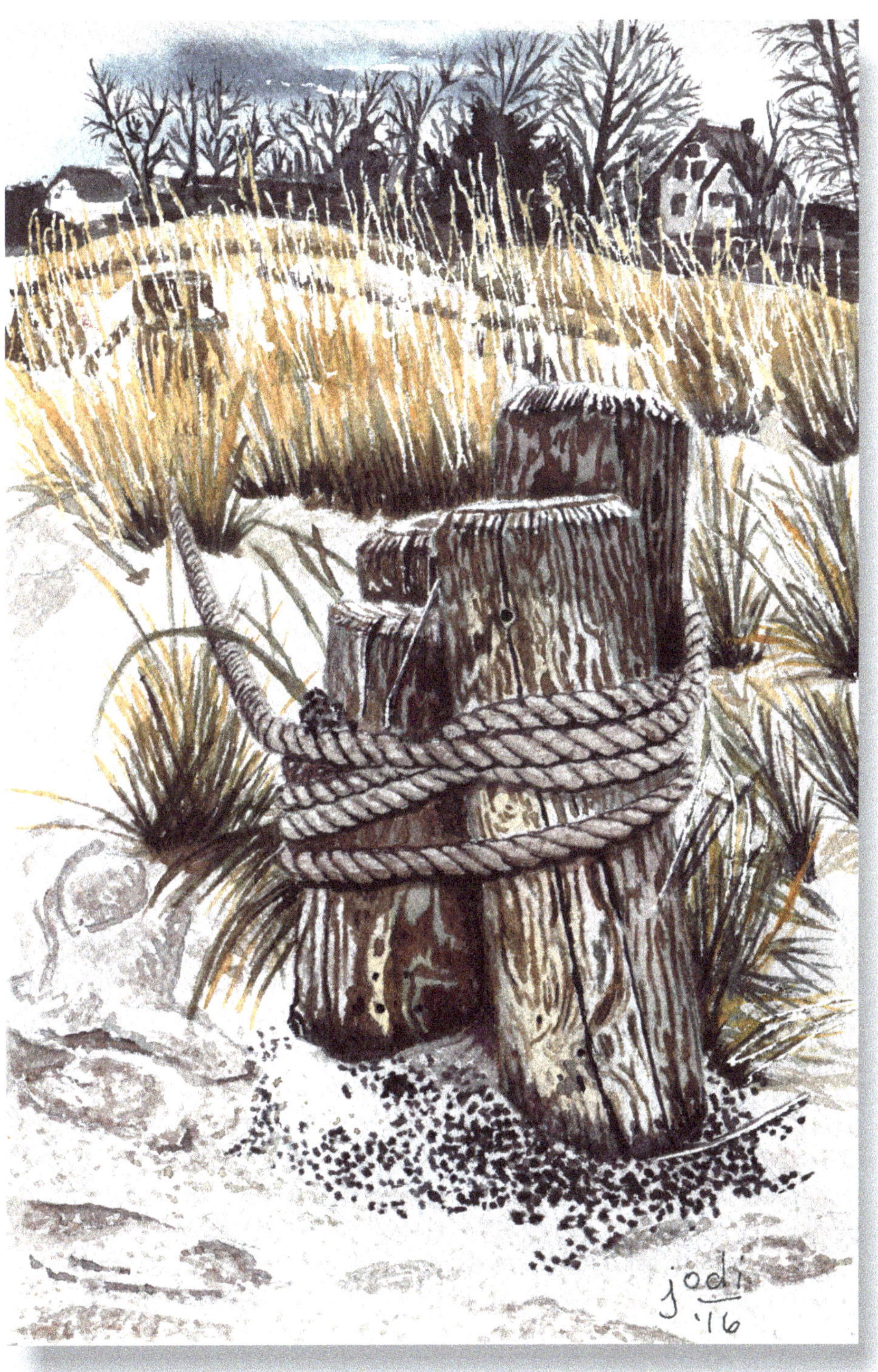
jodi
'16

Sunshine Through My Daisy

This was quite fun. I just loved the colors. Anything that is back-lit takes on a completely different feel. Can't stop learning something new.

Reference photo posted by Dianne Hewitt in Photos For Artists
6 7/8" by 7 1/4" on Arches cold press watercolor paper

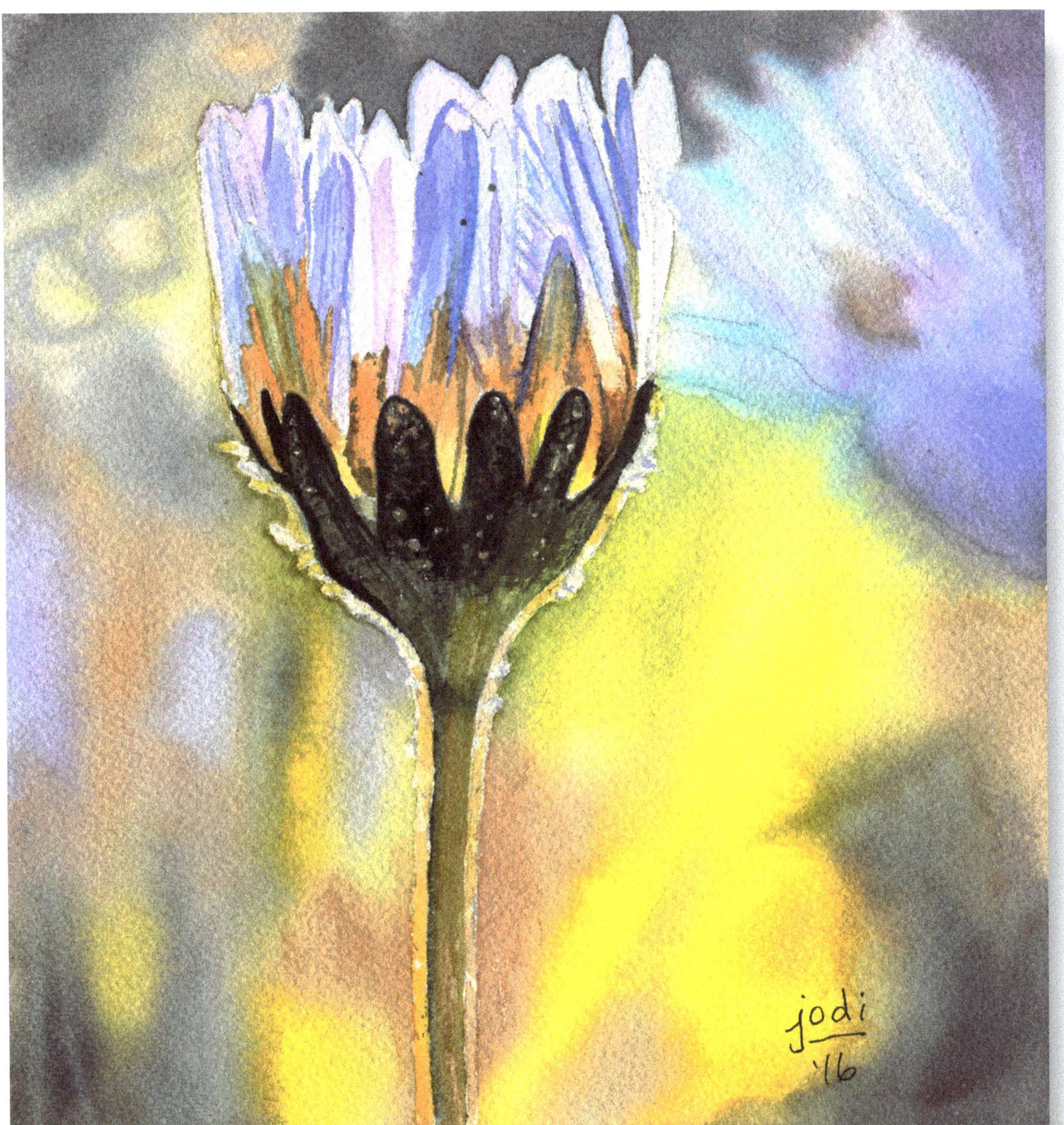
jodi
'16

Hummingbird on Flower Stalk

I seem to gravitate to complicated flowers for some reason. Also this colorful hummingbird intrigued me. Sometimes I amaze myself at the colors I can mix from the three primary colors, as is shown in this painting.

Reference image from Puzzles For Friends
6 1/4" by 9 3/8" on 140 pound Arches cold press watercolor paper

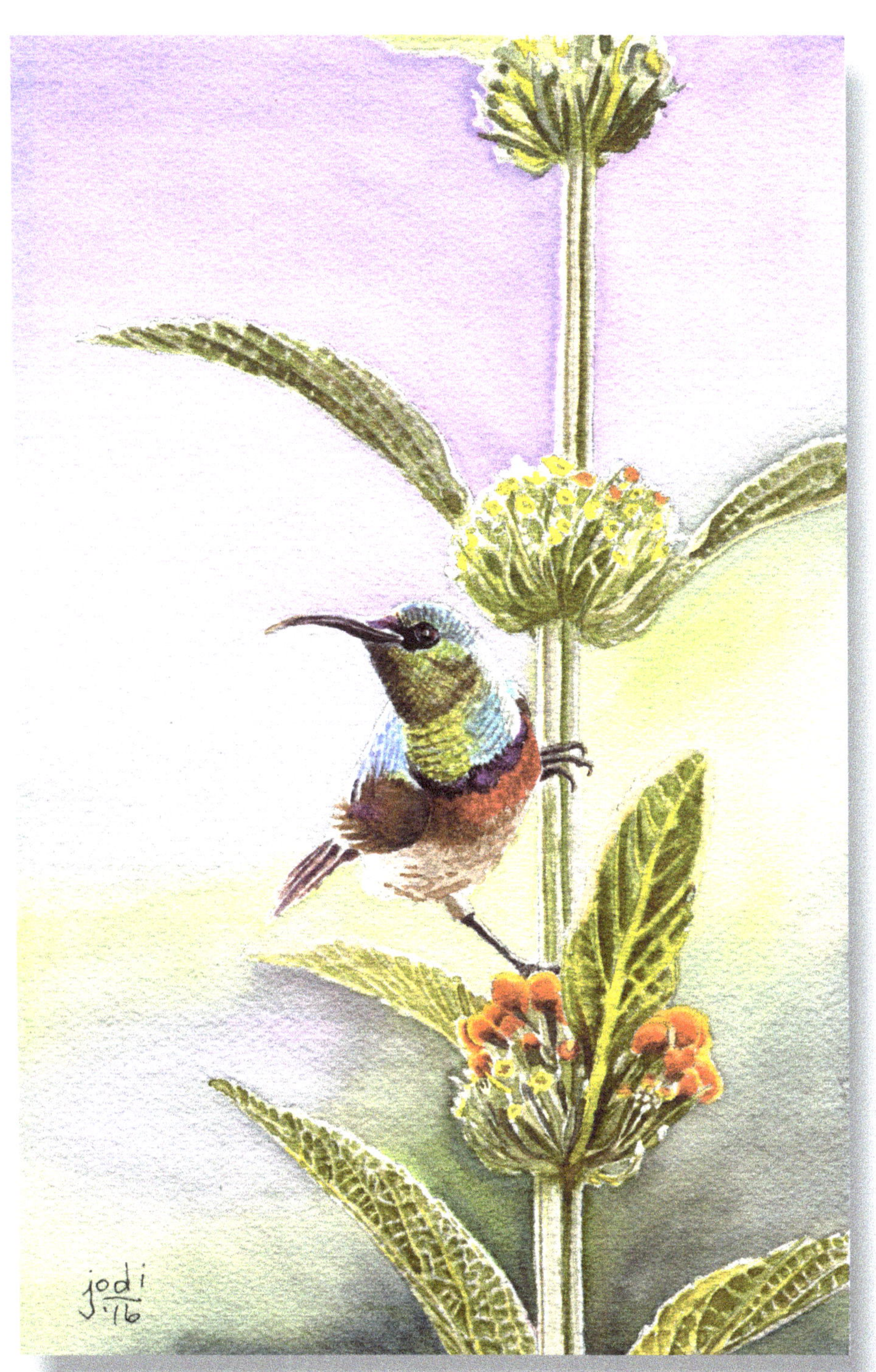
jodi
'16

A Tisket, a Tasket

How could I resist this basket full of apples? The basket weave was great fun and I amazed myself by how simple it was to create.

Reference image from Puzzles For Friends
8 7/8" by 5 5/8" on Arches cold press watercolor paper

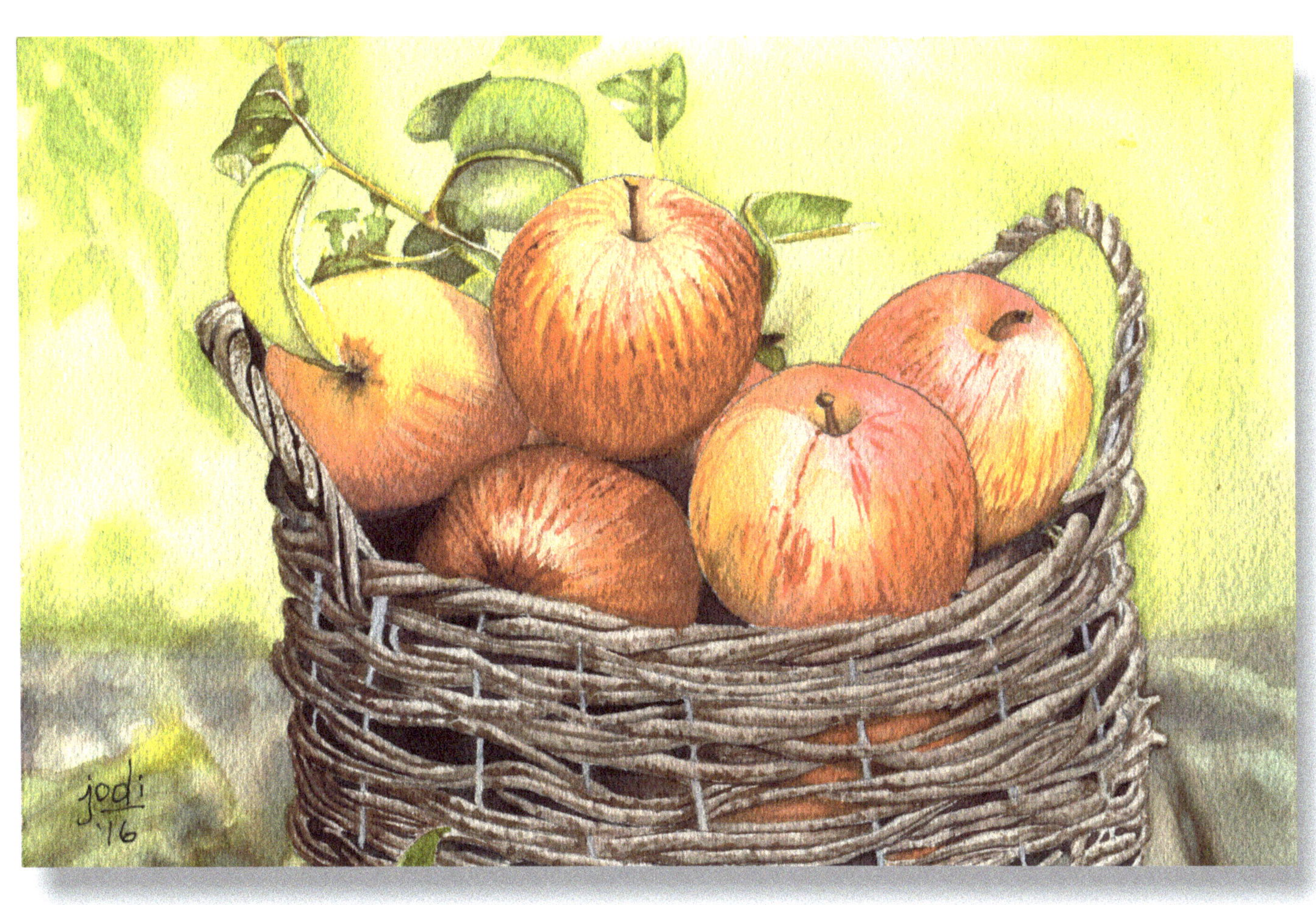
jodi
'16

A Lotus Blossom

An up-close and personal view of a beautiful blossom. Again, no white paint was used in this painting at all. There is just something about a very close-up view of a blossom that is appealing to me.

Reference photo posted by Wendy Sinclair in Photos For Artists
8 1/4" by 5 3/4" on 140 pound Arches cold press watercolor paper

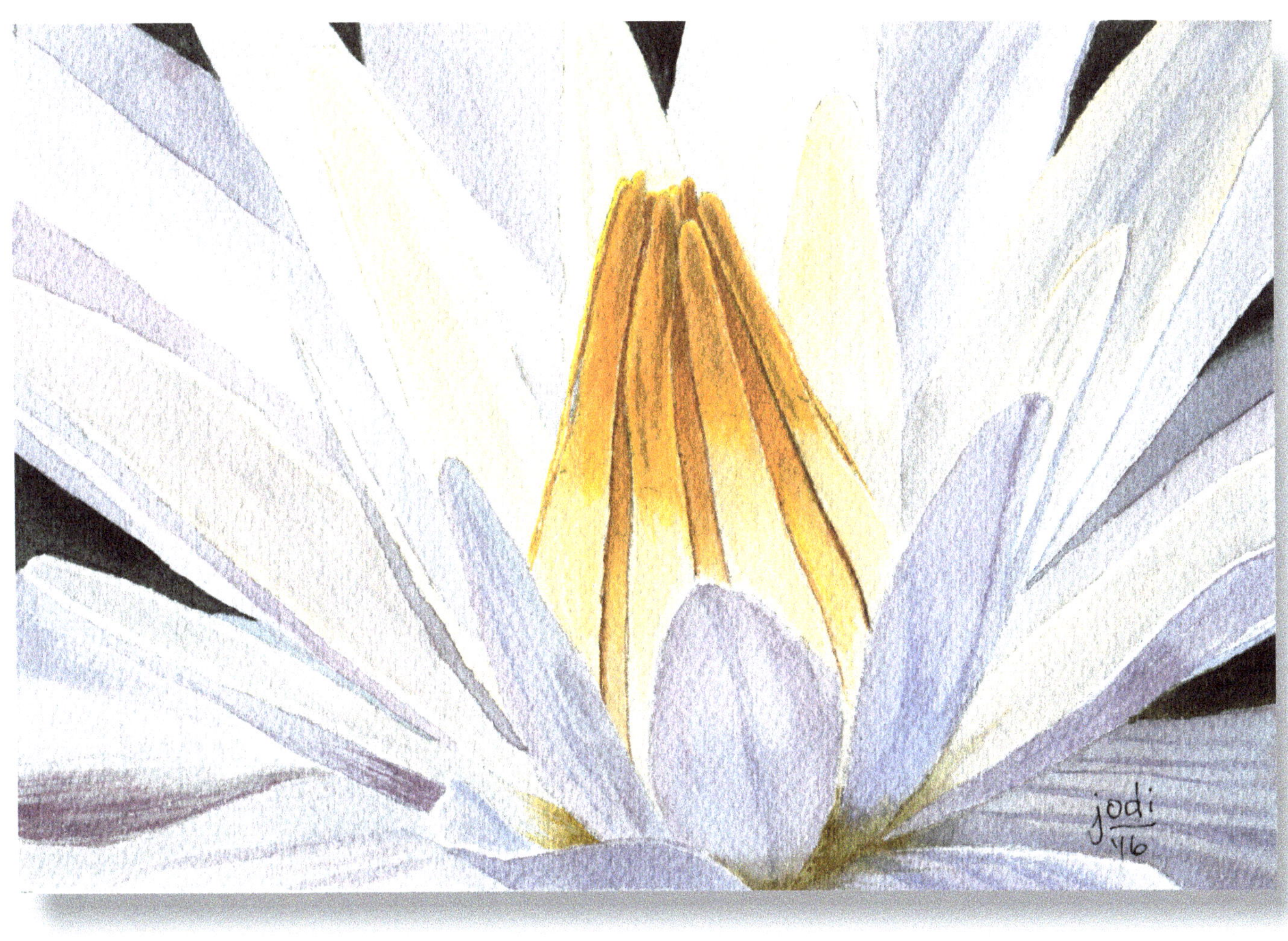
jodi
'16

Swallow Tail on Cosmos

First time I've done a butterfly like this one. In the on-line course I took, I did a close-up of a tiny butterfly. It was so close-up that you could see the little hairs on the wings. This one was much easier and I love the colors of the Swallow Tail anyway.

Image is from Puzzles For Friends
7' by 4 3/4" on 140 pound Arches cold press watercolor paper

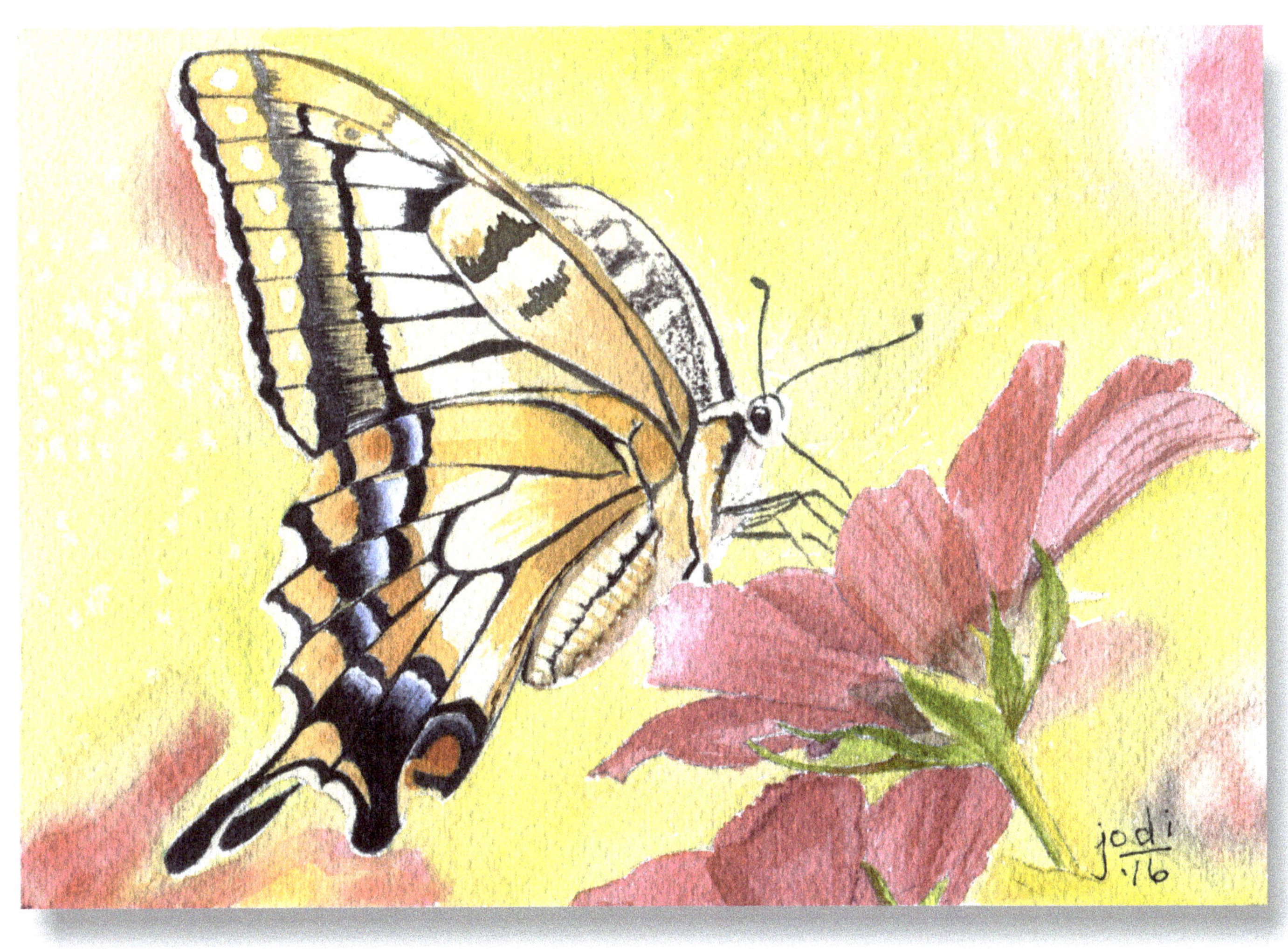
jodi
'16

Green Boat Reflection

This was so much fun, actually. You can see in this one that I am getting a bit more comfortable doing water. Seems like it is always different in every situation.

Reference photo by Bernard Geraghty in Photos For Artists
7" by 6 1/4" on Arches cold press watercolor paper

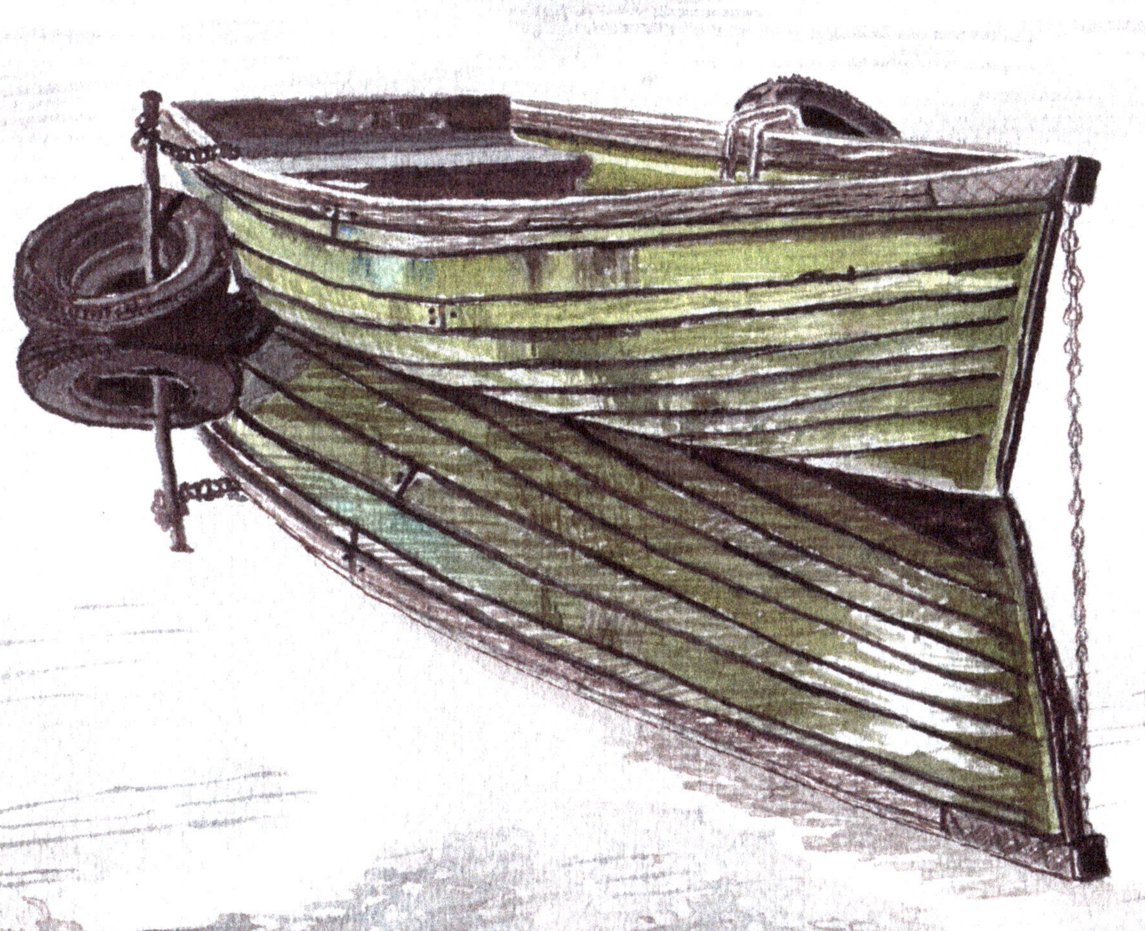
jodi
'16

Koi Fish

This took me about a week, off and on, to paint. Every part of it was a challenge and it turned out to be my favorite of every piece I've painted. Remember, no black nor white was used in this. All colors are mixed from the three primary colors.

Reference photo by Colin Banks in Photos For Artists
6 7/8" by 8 5/8" on 140 pound Arches cold press watercolor paper

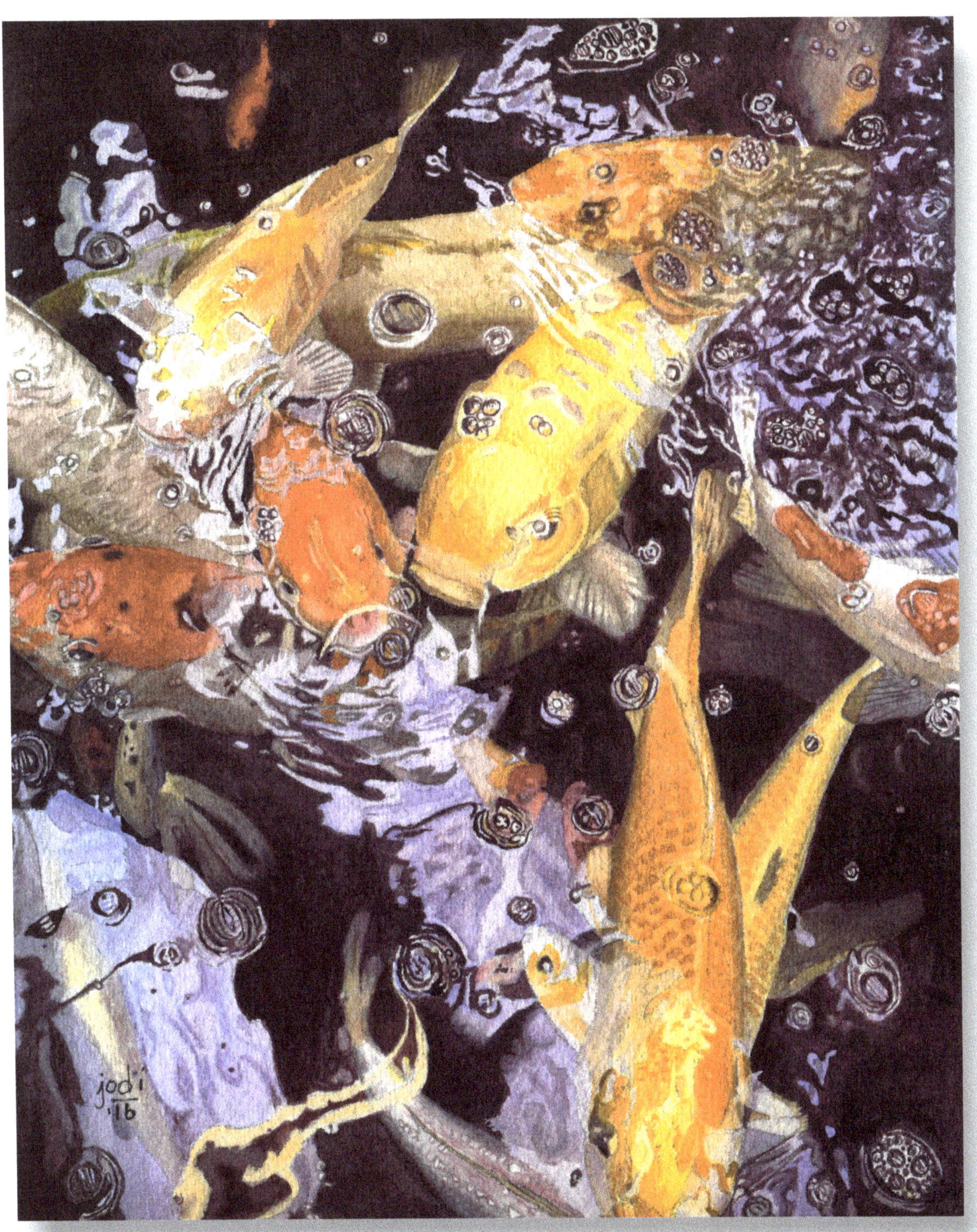
jodi
'16

Red Yarrow

The scientific name for this plant is Achillea millefolium, commonly known as yarrow /gordaldo/ or common yarrow, and it is a flowering plant in the family Asteraceae. It is native to temperate regions of the Northern Hemisphere in Asia, Europe, and North America. Not sure which variety this is but may be 'paprika'. I love botanical painting and someday hope to do a book of paintings of the indigenous plants of Oregon.

Painted by invitation from Kathleen Gilchrist Garrels who took the reference photo
5" by 7 1/2" on 140 pound Arches cold press watercolor paper

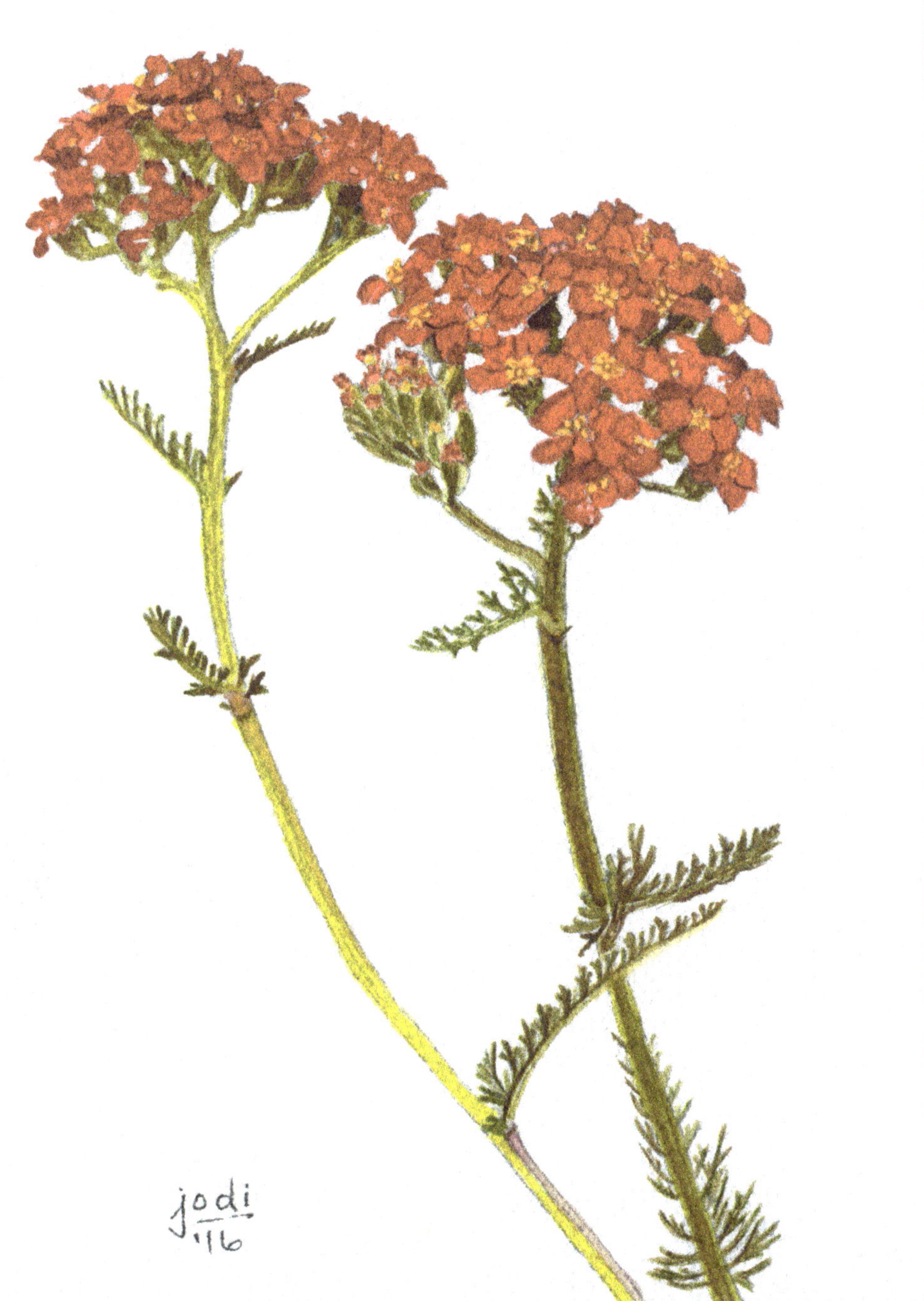
jodi
'16

Green Eyed Cat

Just had to do this for the eyes. I love doing eyes and fur. It is so much fun for an artist. Again, let me remind you that there is no white nor black paint used in this painting.

Reference image from Puzzles For Friends
6 7/8" square on Arches 140 pound cold press watercolor paper

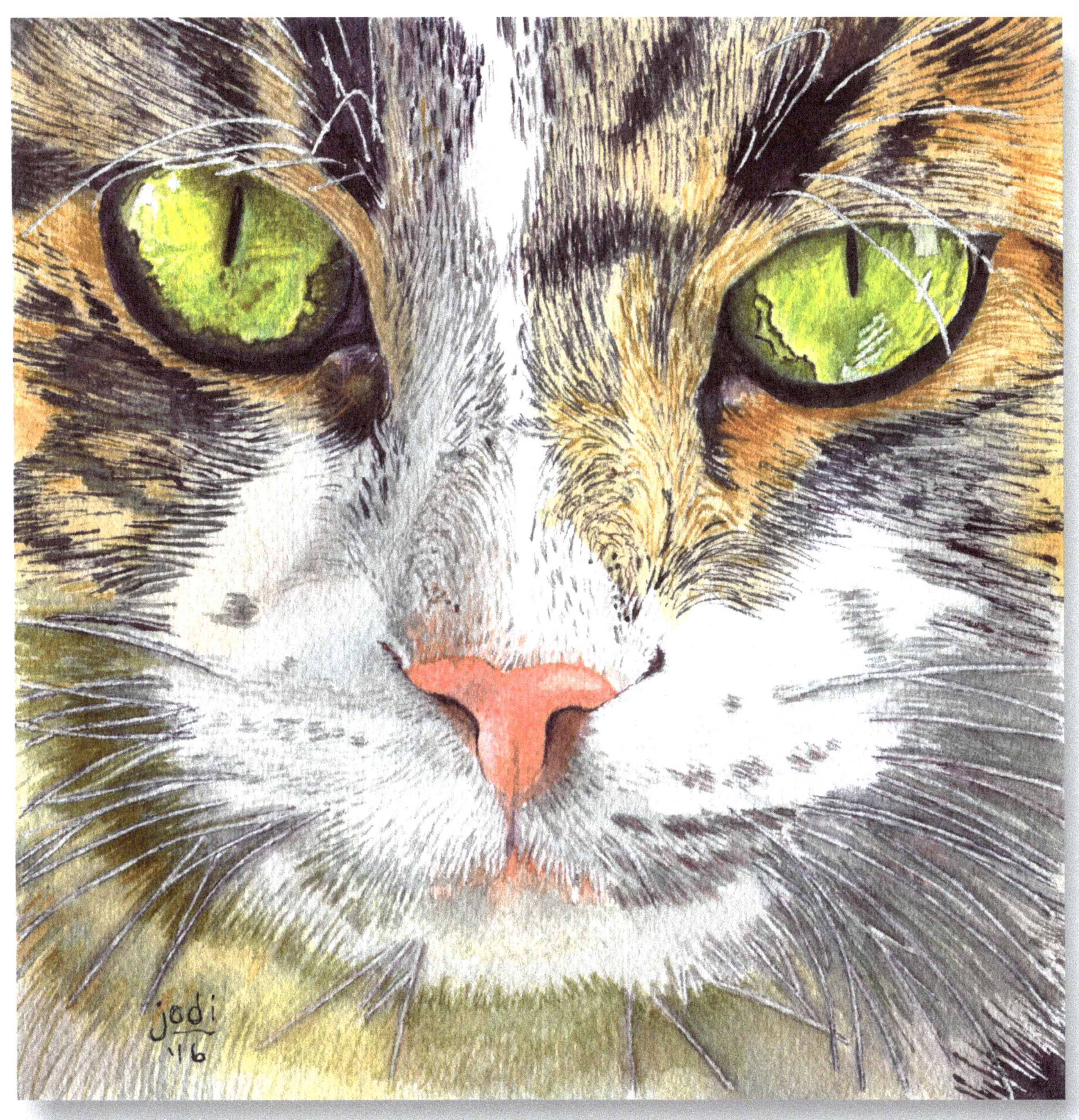
jodi
'16

Cross-eyed Owl

How could I not paint this cute Owl? I don't think it is really cross-eyed. What I think is actually going on here is that it is looking directly at the viewer which gives it a kind of cross-eyed look. Too cute.

Reference image from Puzzles For Friends
8 1/4" by 6 1/8" on Arches 140 pound cold press watercolor paper

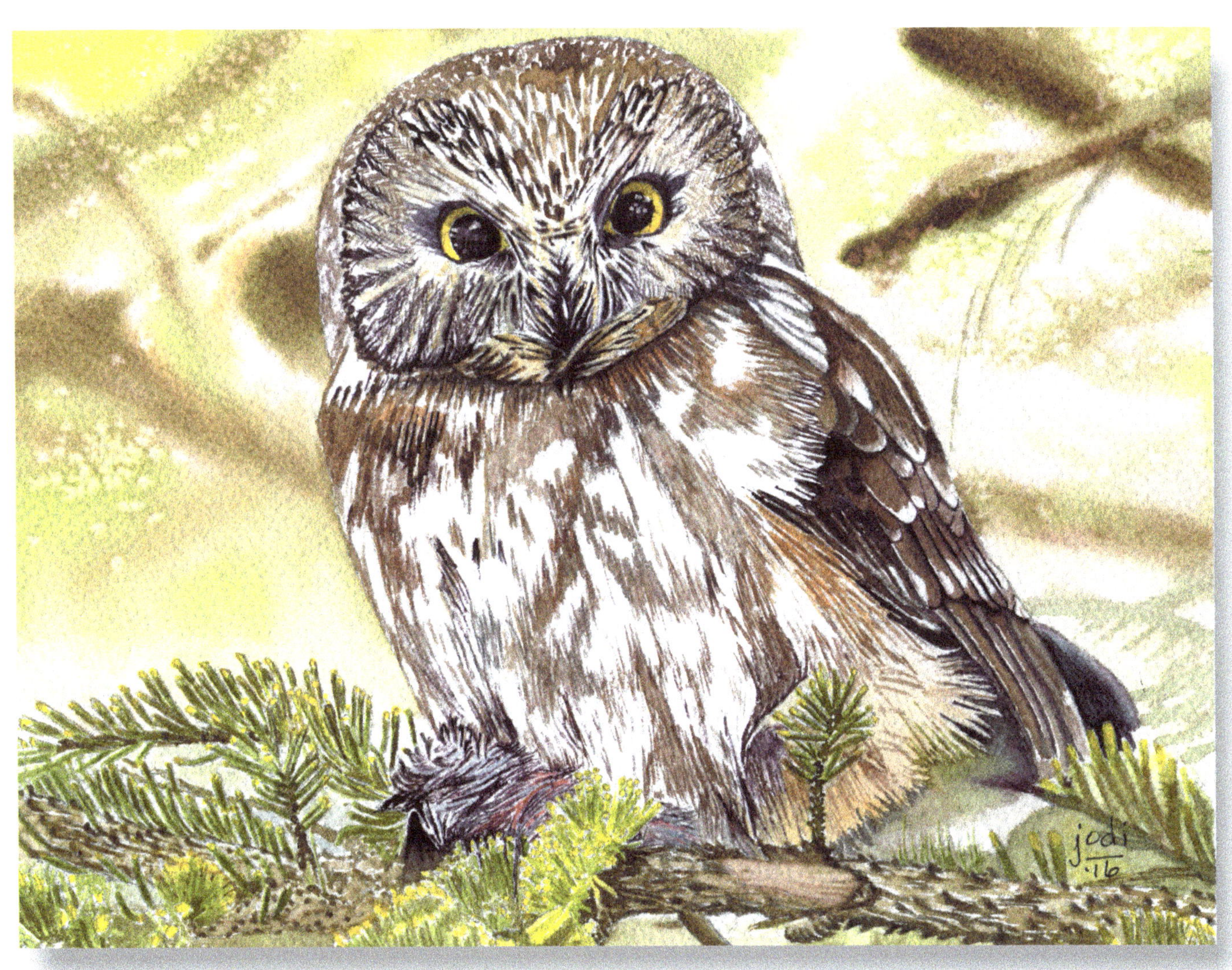
jodi
'16

Honey Bee on Yellow Flowers

Here I go with the weird flowers. Seems like they are like a magnet to me. I did a close-up of a honey bee in the on-line class I took, so just wanted to do another. Their hairy bodies are just up my alley.

Image from an "inhabitat" photo
8 1/4" by 5 3/8" on Arches 140 pound cold press watercolor paper

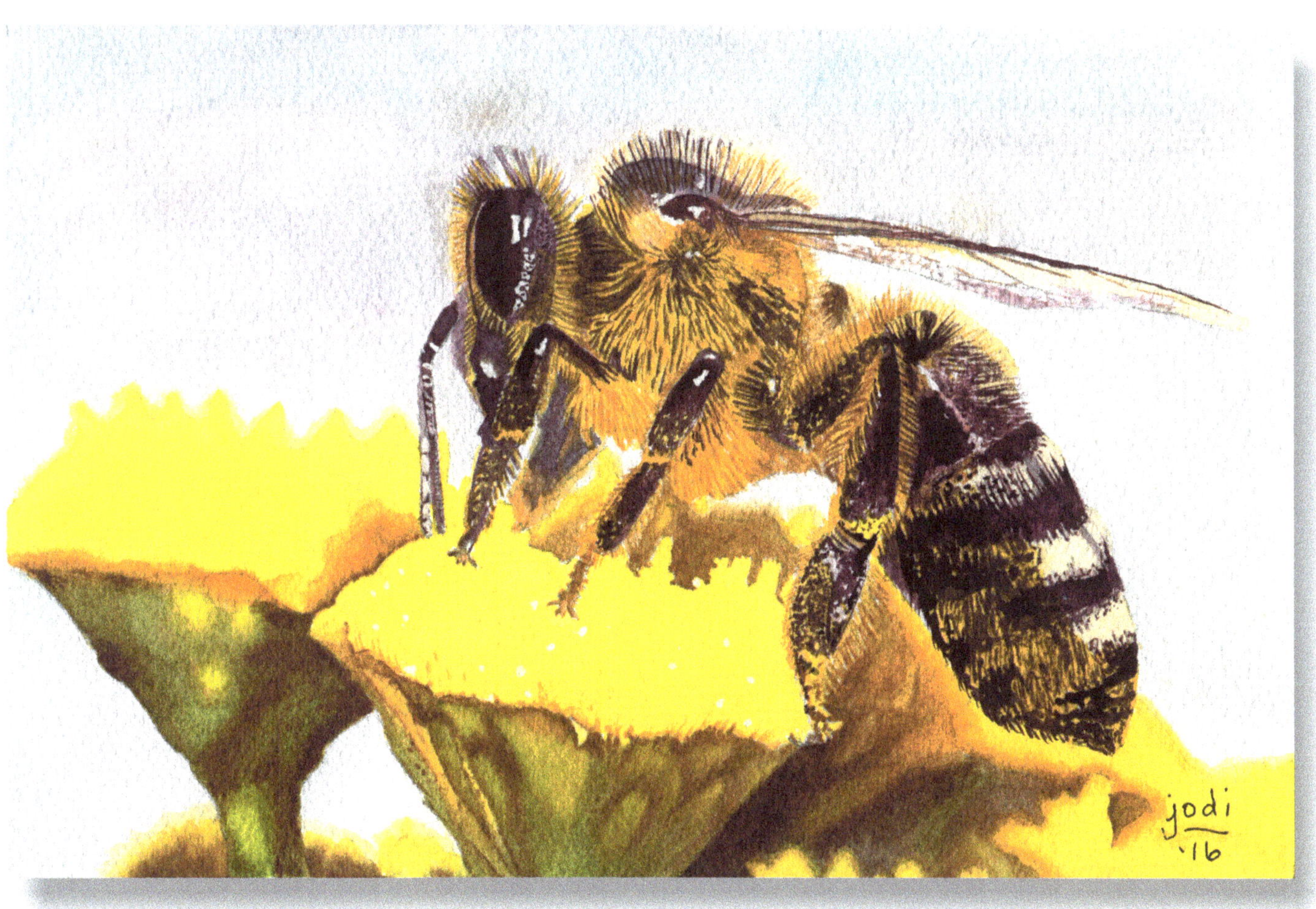
jodi
'16

Lily-of-the-Valley

I took this photo in my own yard just after a light rain. The rain drops sat on the leaves just like diamonds that looked like they weren't even touching the surface.

Reference photo by artist
7" by 9 1/4" on Arches 140 pound cold press watercolor paper

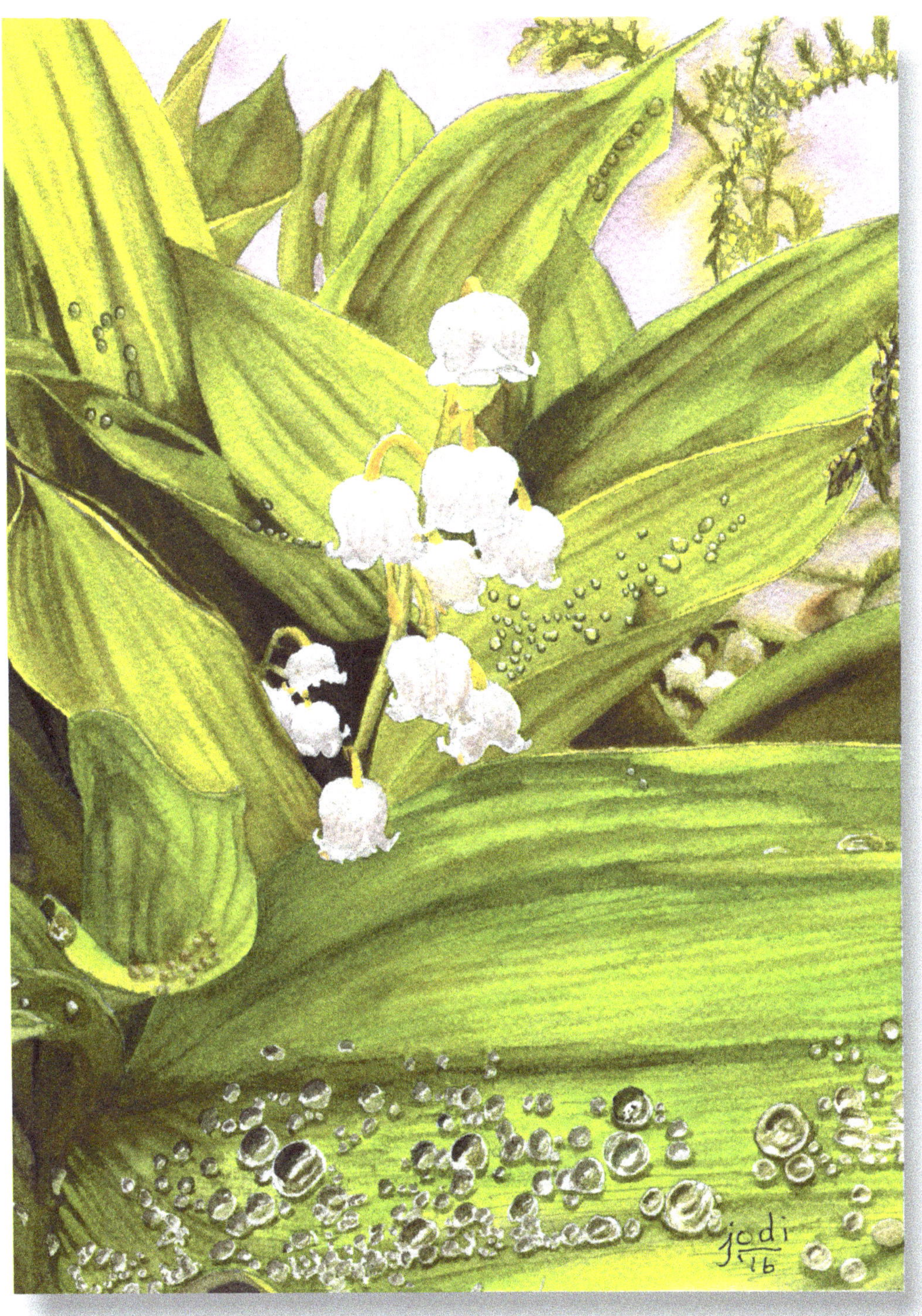
jodi
'16

Yellow Water Lilies

I painted this from a photo I took at Oregon Gardens in Silverton, Oregon. We try to get there at least every other year for my husband's birthday. Being in April, many things are in bloom at that time. A great place and a perfect time of year to go.

Reference photo by artist
8 1/4" by 6 1/4" on Arches 140 pound cold press watercolor paper

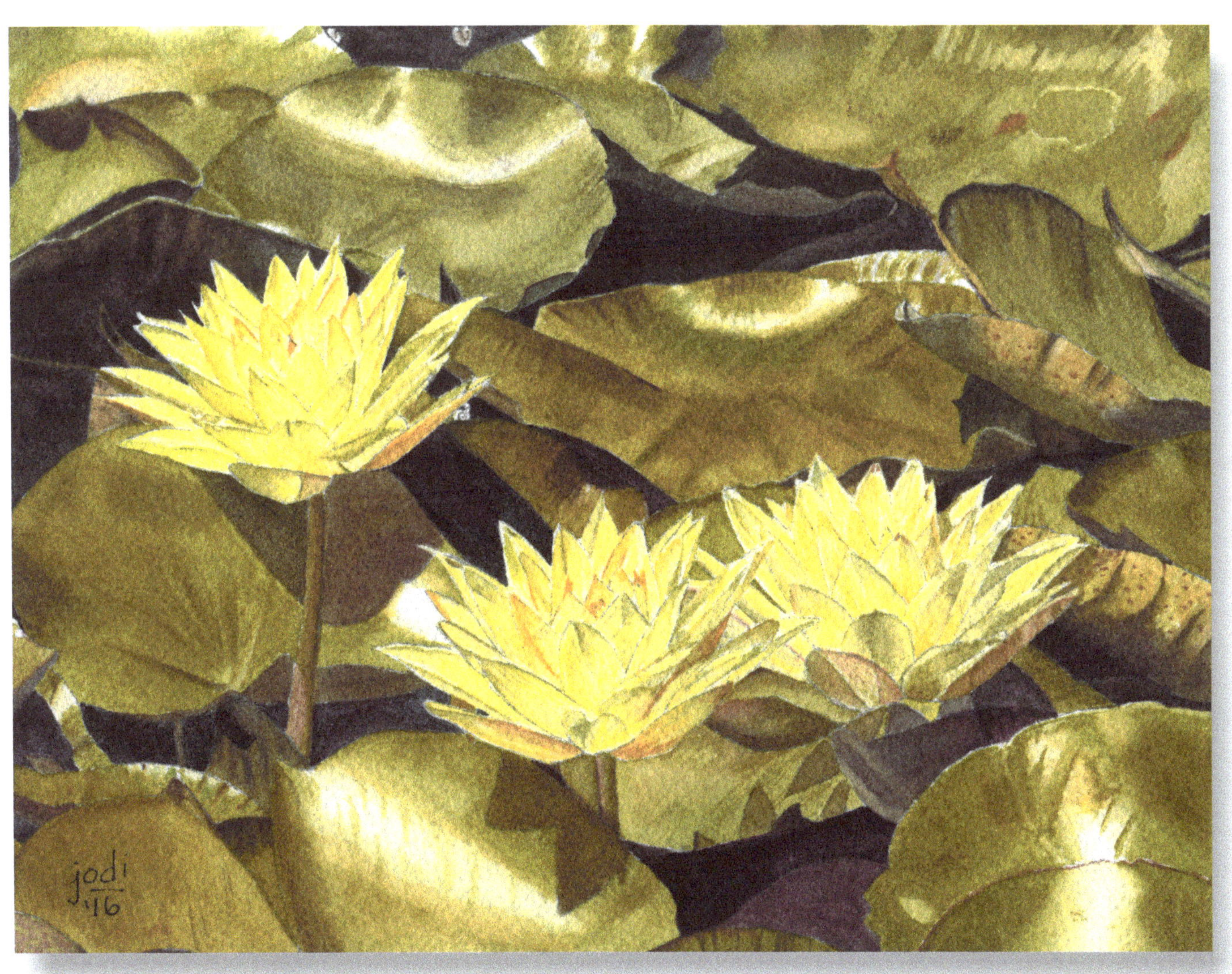
jodi
'16

Poinsettia

Red Poinsettia's are my favorite Christmas plant. The red are actually the leaves that turn red near the tiny yellow flowers at the center. All Poinsettia's have yellow flowers, but the leaves near them can be different colors. There is nothing that says "Christmas" more to me than red, so I did use this as a Christmas card one year.

Reference image inspired from Anna Mason's on-line tutorial
8 1/2" by 7" on Fabriano cold press watercolor paper

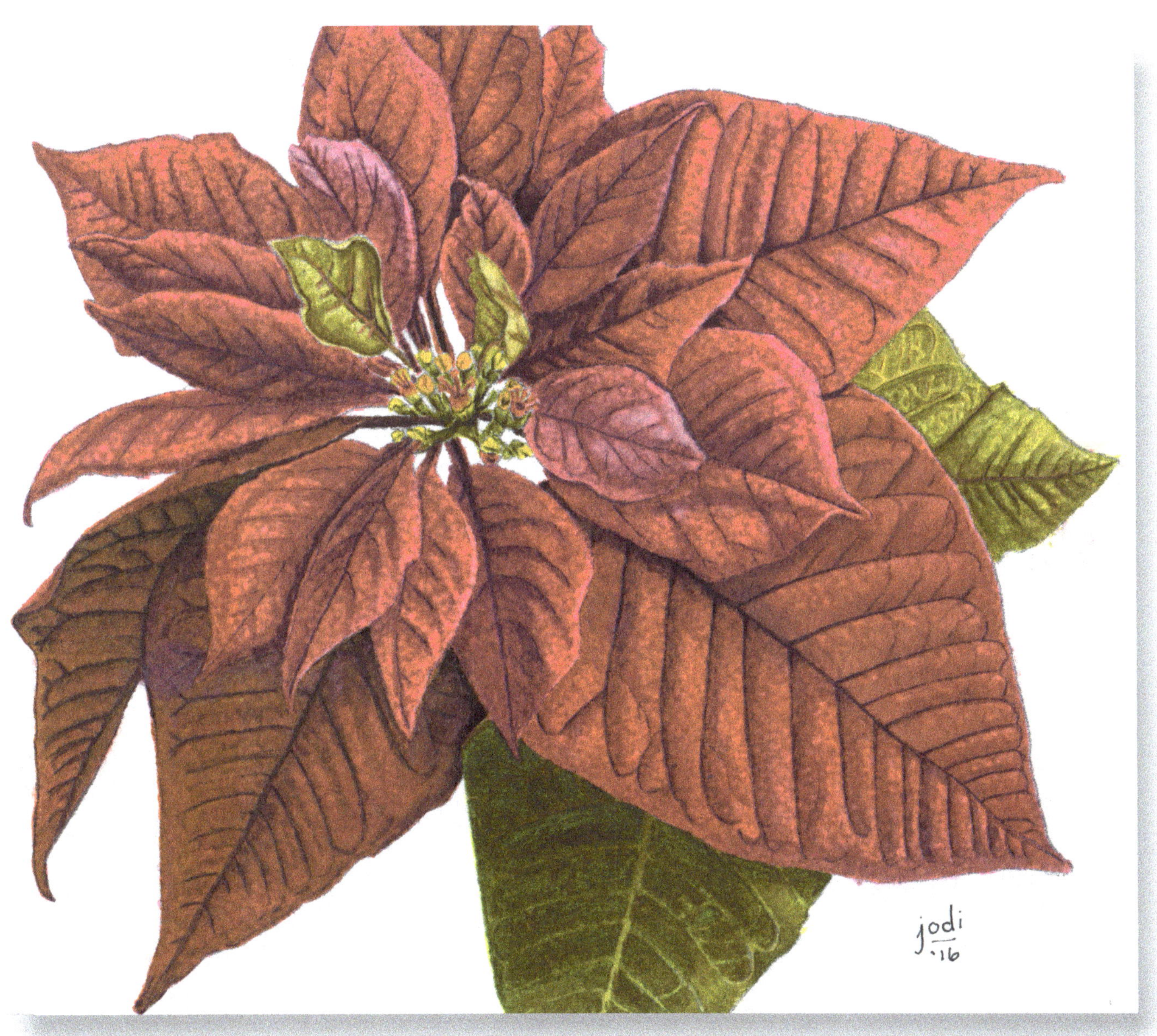
jodi
'16

Rainbow Peacock Feather

Well, what can I say? I love rainbow things and anything with lots of color. I guess this is just my inner-child coming out.

Reference image from Puzzles for Friends
3 7/8" by 5 1/4" on Strathmore 140 pound cold press watercolor paper

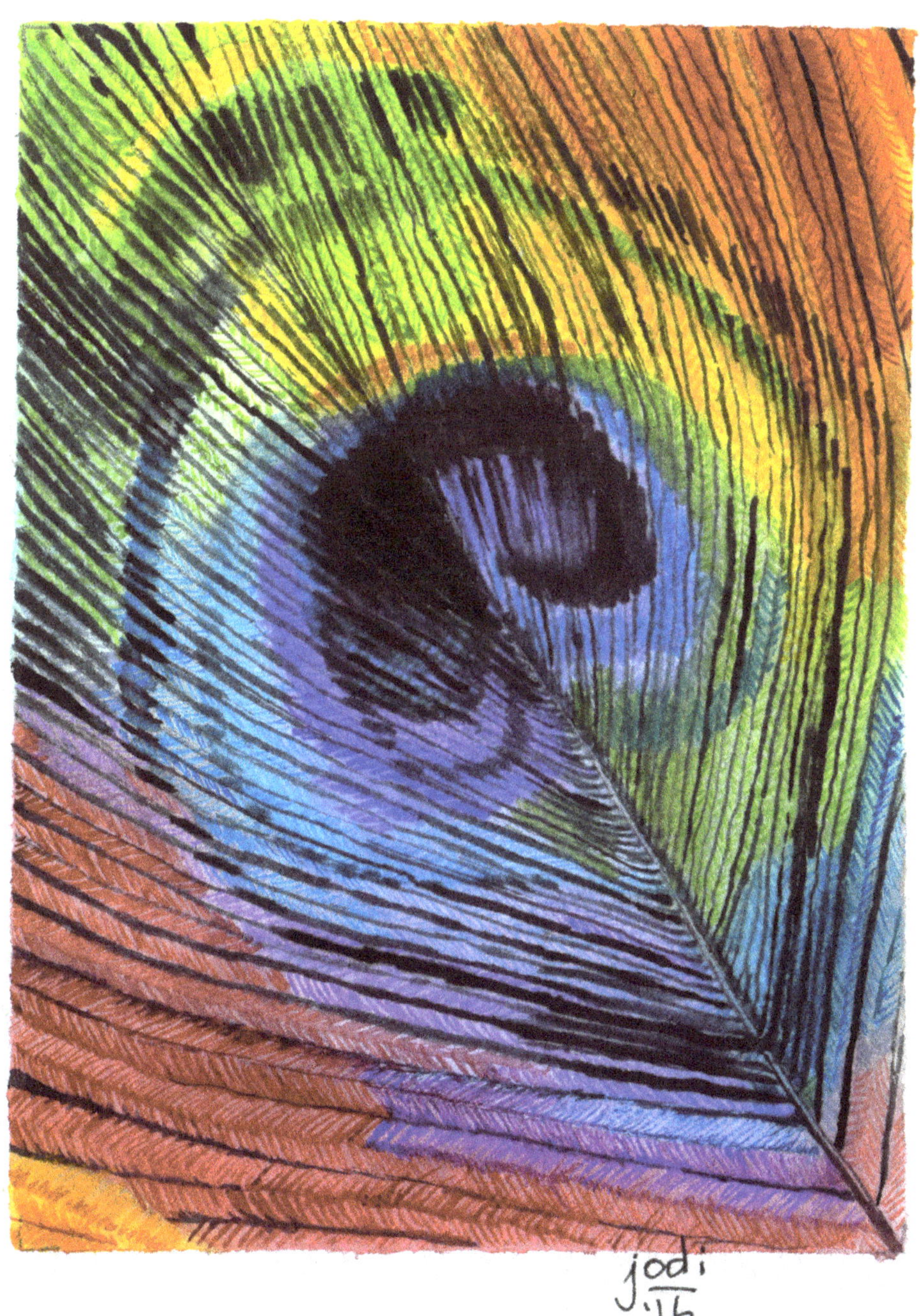
jodi
'16

Peace in the Midst of the Storm

Credit to the web for inspiration on this one. I just had to do a relatively easy one for a change. This is the easiest painting I've ever done and I really enjoyed its simplicity.

Reference image from Pinterest
5 1/4" by 7 1/4" on Fabriano cold press watercolor paper

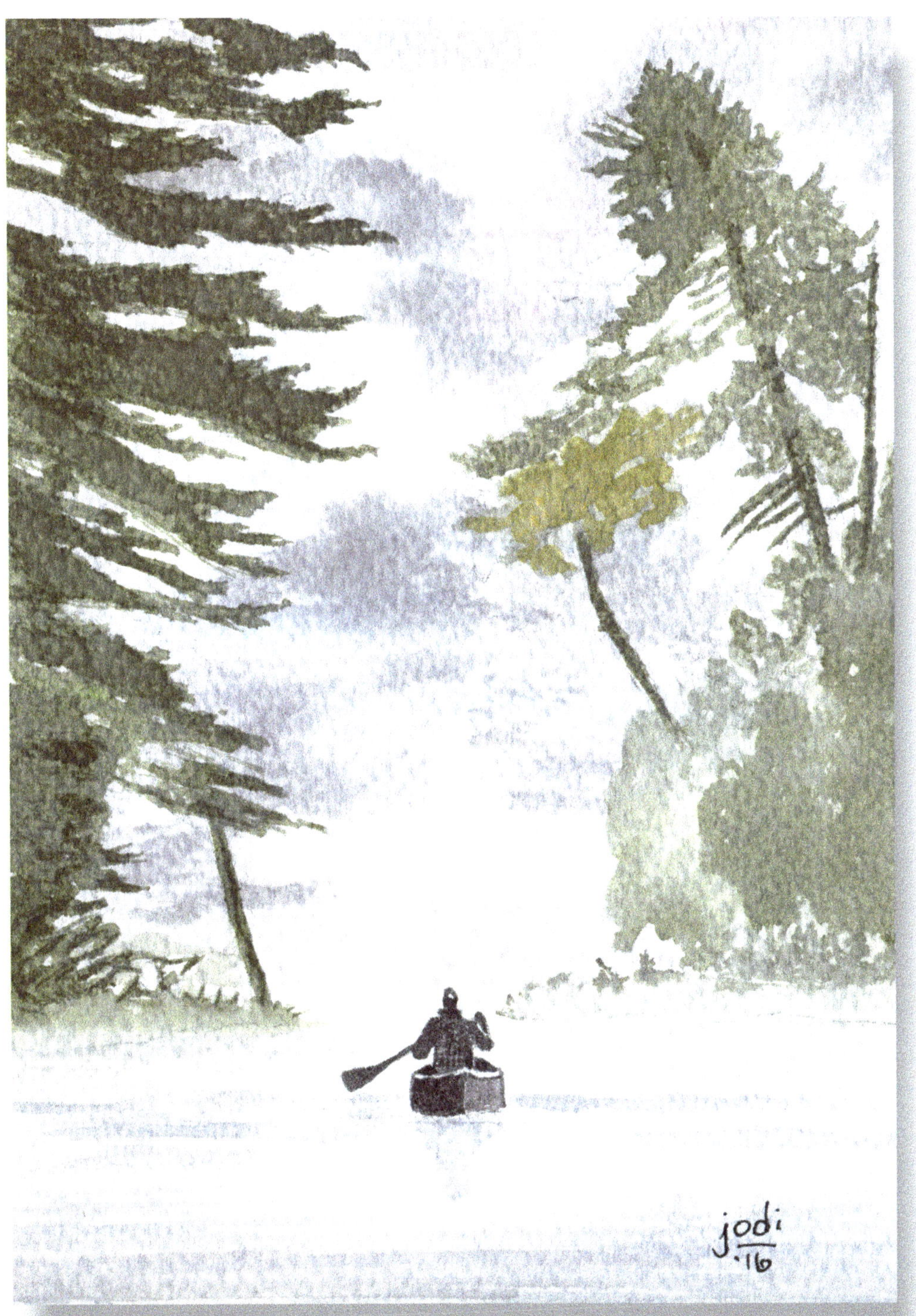
jodi
'16

The Red Fox

Here I go with the fur again. Feathers and fur are so much fun to paint. I got this image from the jig-saw puzzles I used to play on FaceBook.

Reference image from Puzzles For Friends
9 5/8" by 6" on Arches 140 pound cold press watercolor paper

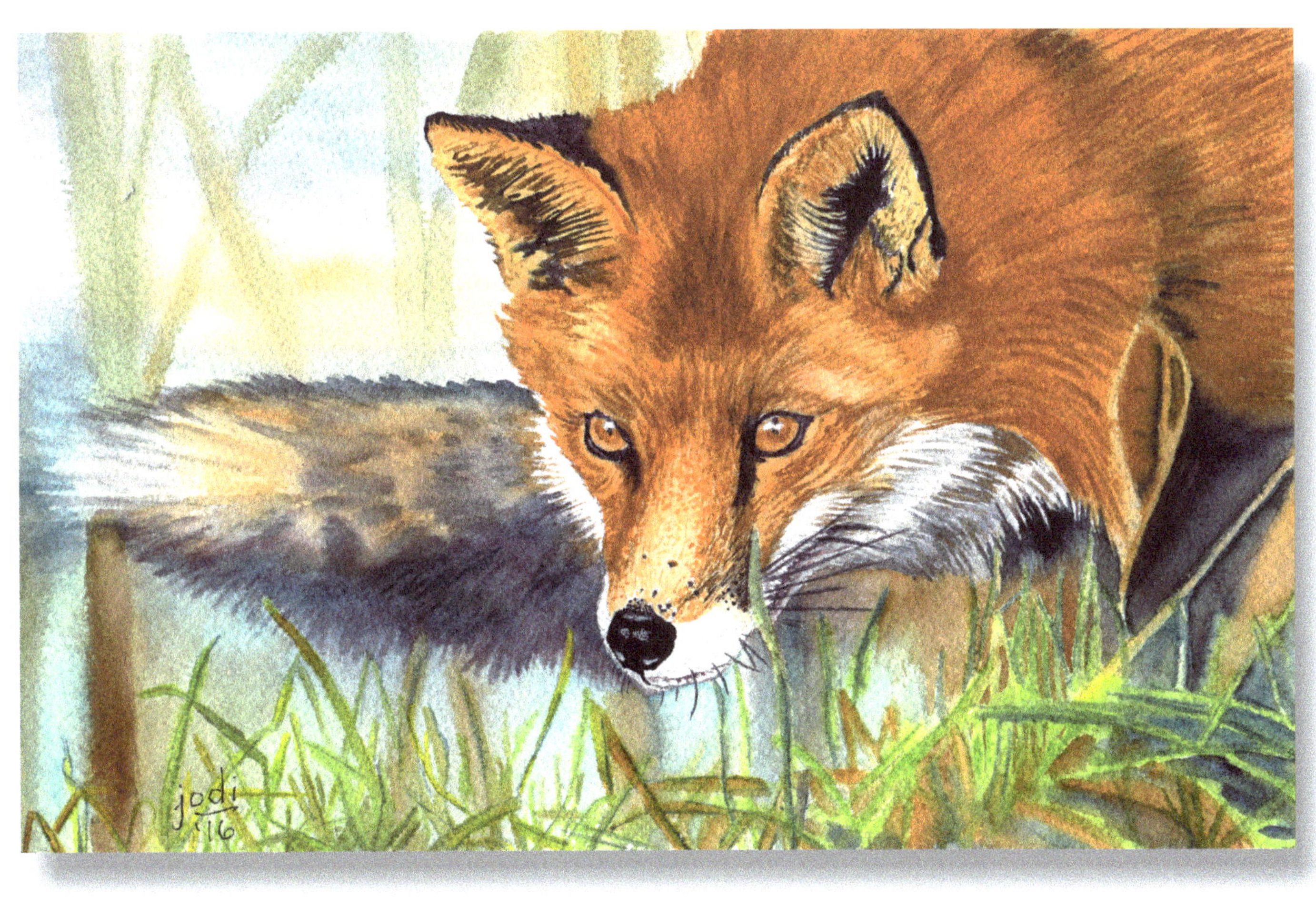
jodi
'16

The Rooster

I did this as a study for another painting I wanted to do for a friend. The iridescence of the feathers were a challenge. As you can see, I am getting pretty good at getting a good black from the three primaries.

Based on a photo by Hugashrimp in Paint My Photo
4 1/2" by 5 1/2 " on Strathmore 140 pound cold press watercolor paper

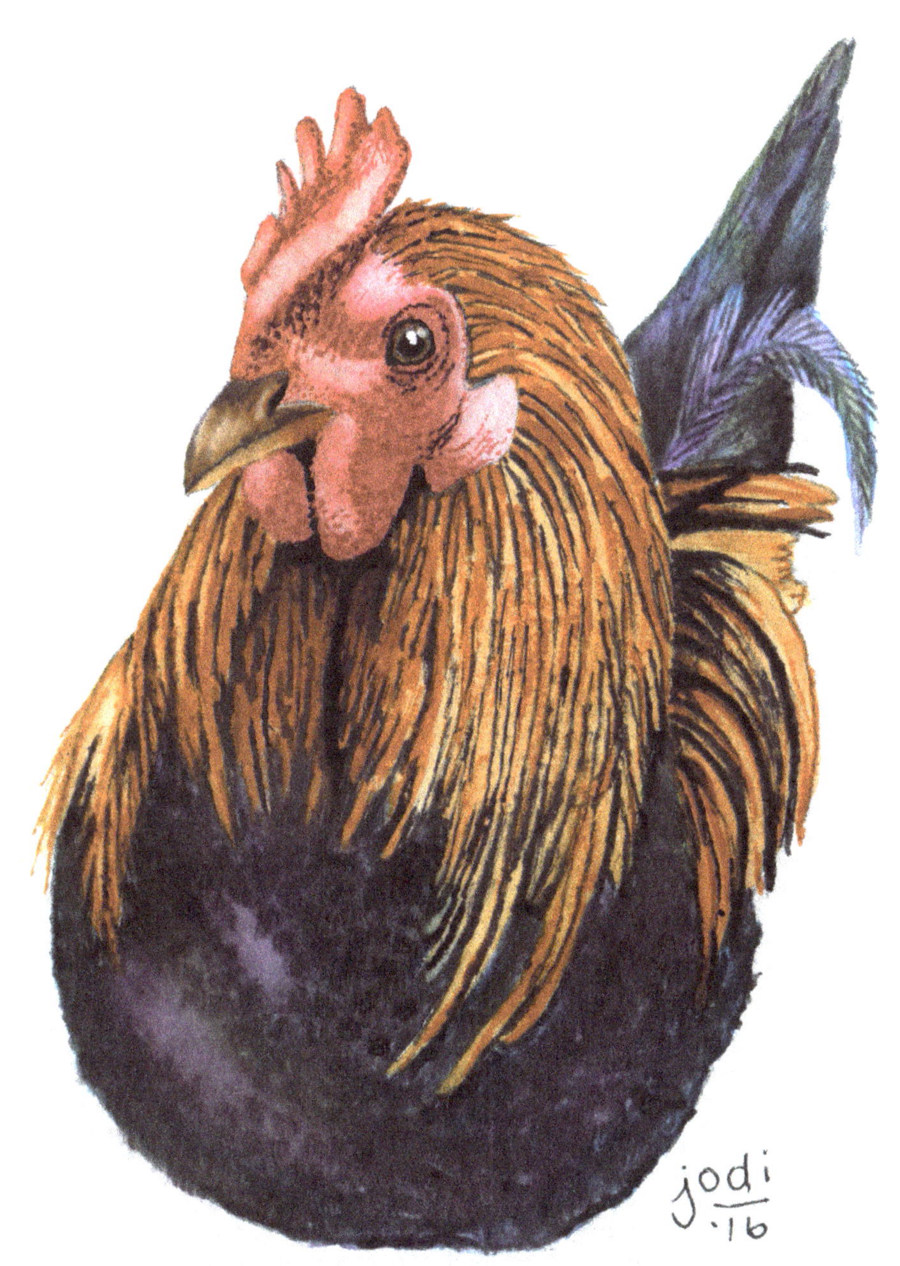
jodi
'16

Heron Silhouette on Lake

Needing a very simple painting to relax, I did this one. I liked how, even with the effects of the silhouettes, you can still make out the different vegetation in this painting. Also I just love the feeling I got from the Heron, one of my favorite waterfowls.

Reference image from Puzzles For Friends
8 7/8" by 6" on Arches 140 pound cold press watercolor paper

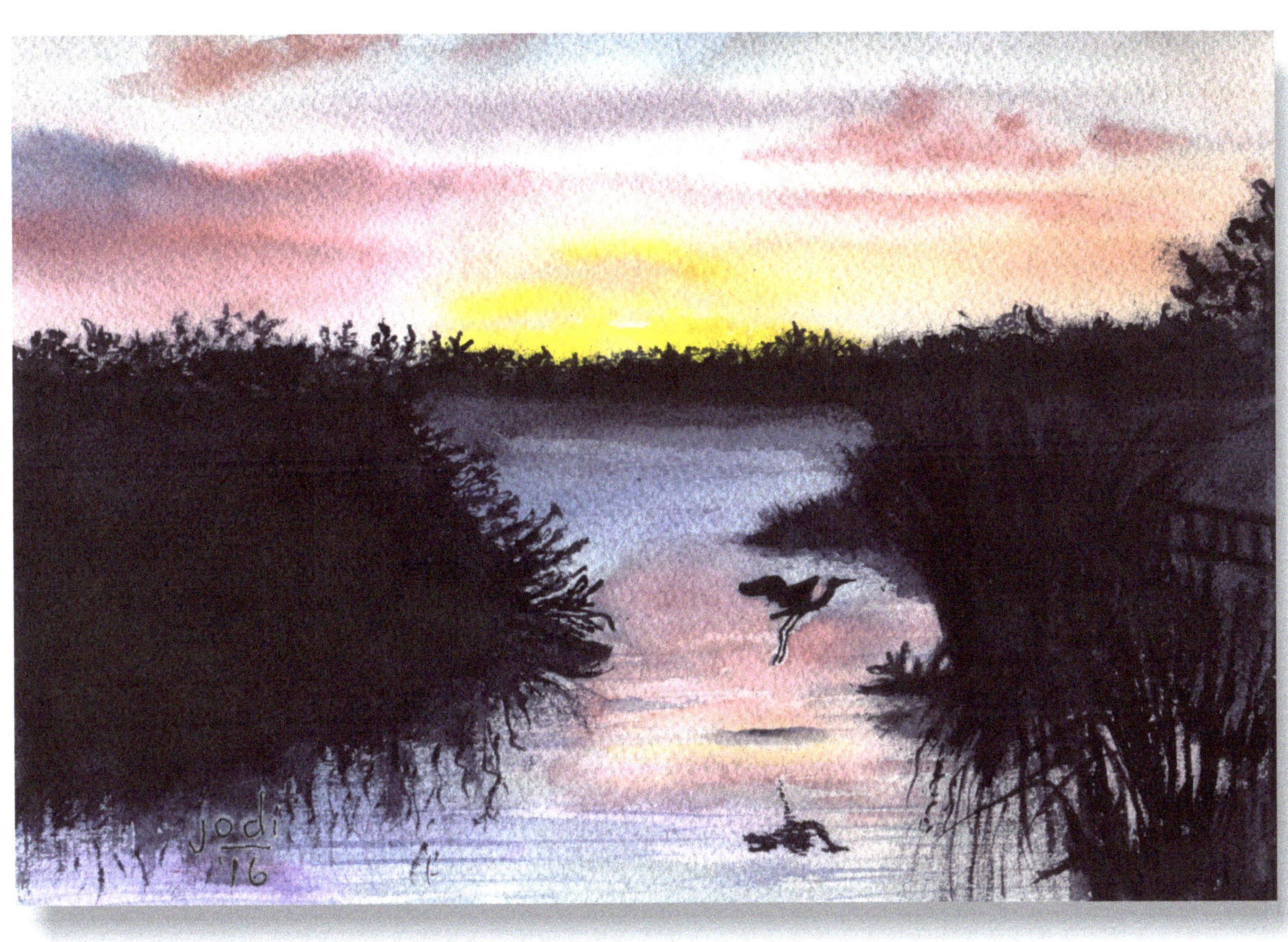
Jodi
'16

Hummingbird with Foxglove

I did this painting from two pictures I put together. Again with my colorful bird and the pink of the foxglove, two of my favorite things.

Hummingbird image from Puzzles For Friends
Foxglove image from the web
9 1/2" by 6 1/4" on Fabriano cold press watercolor paper

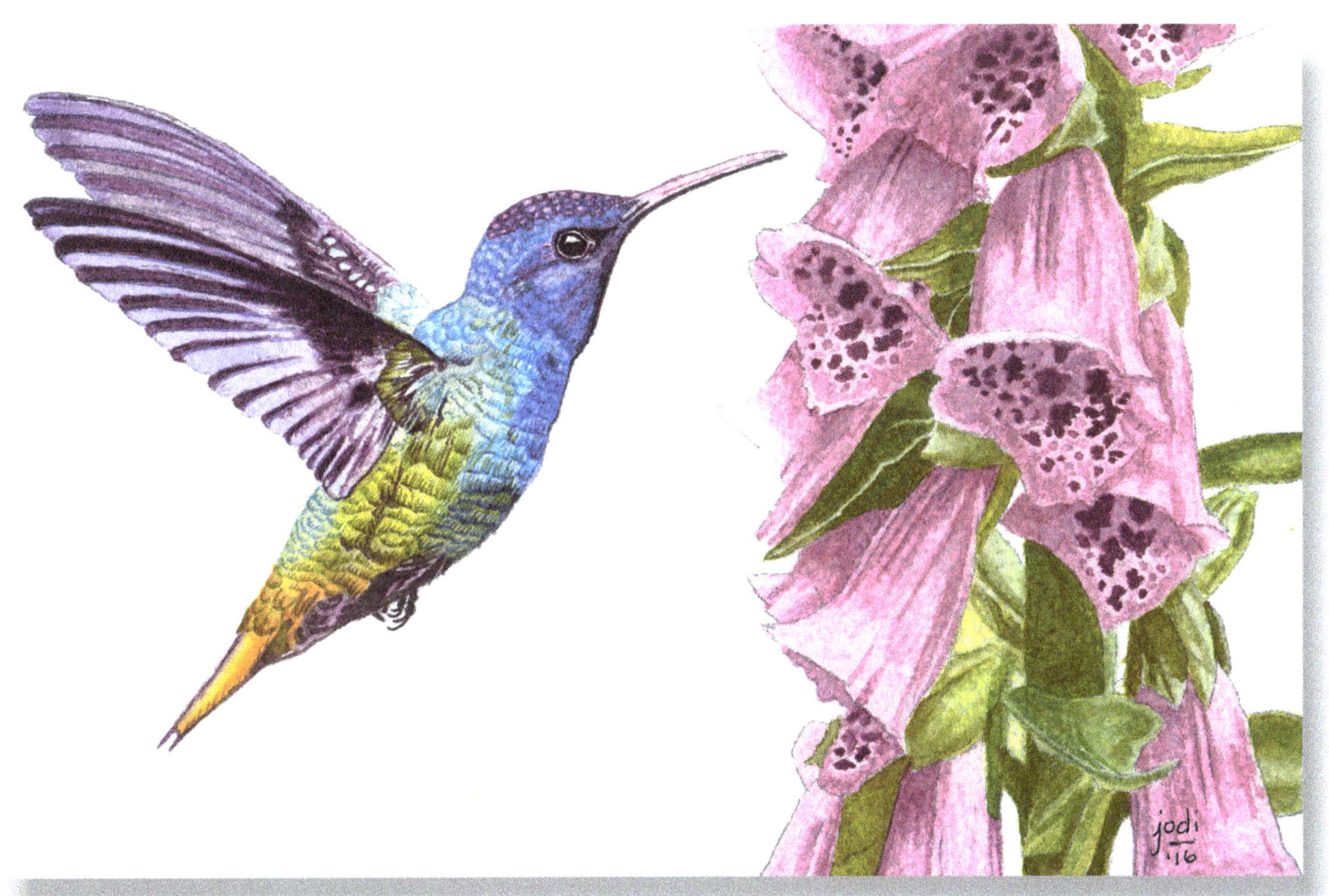
jodi
'16

Kiwi

I love Kiwi. Just couldn't resist this one. The fur of the skin (again with my fur thing) and the juicy flesh of the fruit. A very nice combination.

Reference image from Puzzles For Friends
7" by 4 1/4" on Strathmore 140 pound cold press watercolor paper

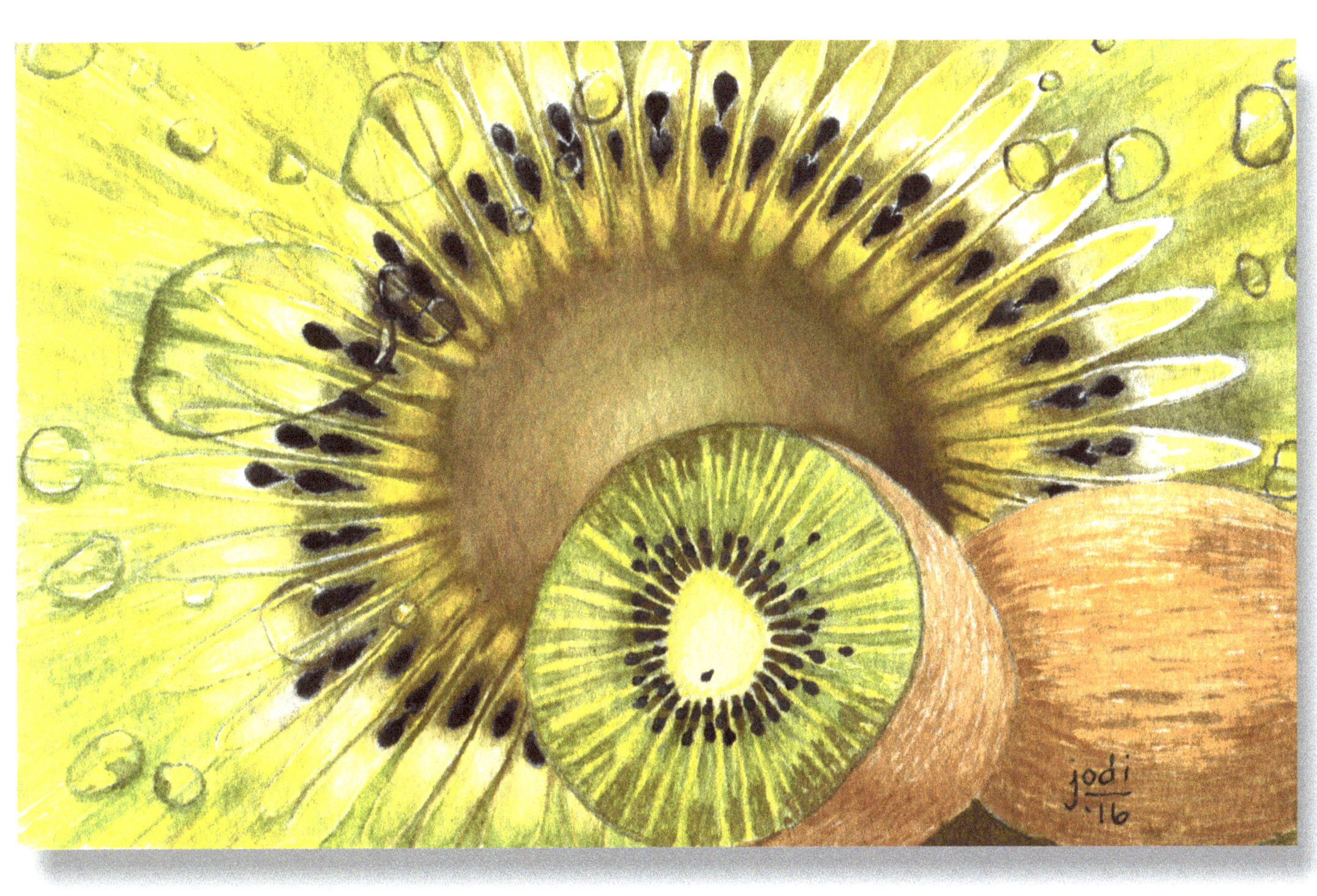
jodi
'16

Frog in Anemone

Now just how could I resist this cute image? This one gave me more color mixing challenges. Everything is a learning curve for me.

Reference image from Puzzles For Friends
7" by 6" on Arches 140 pound cold press watercolor paper

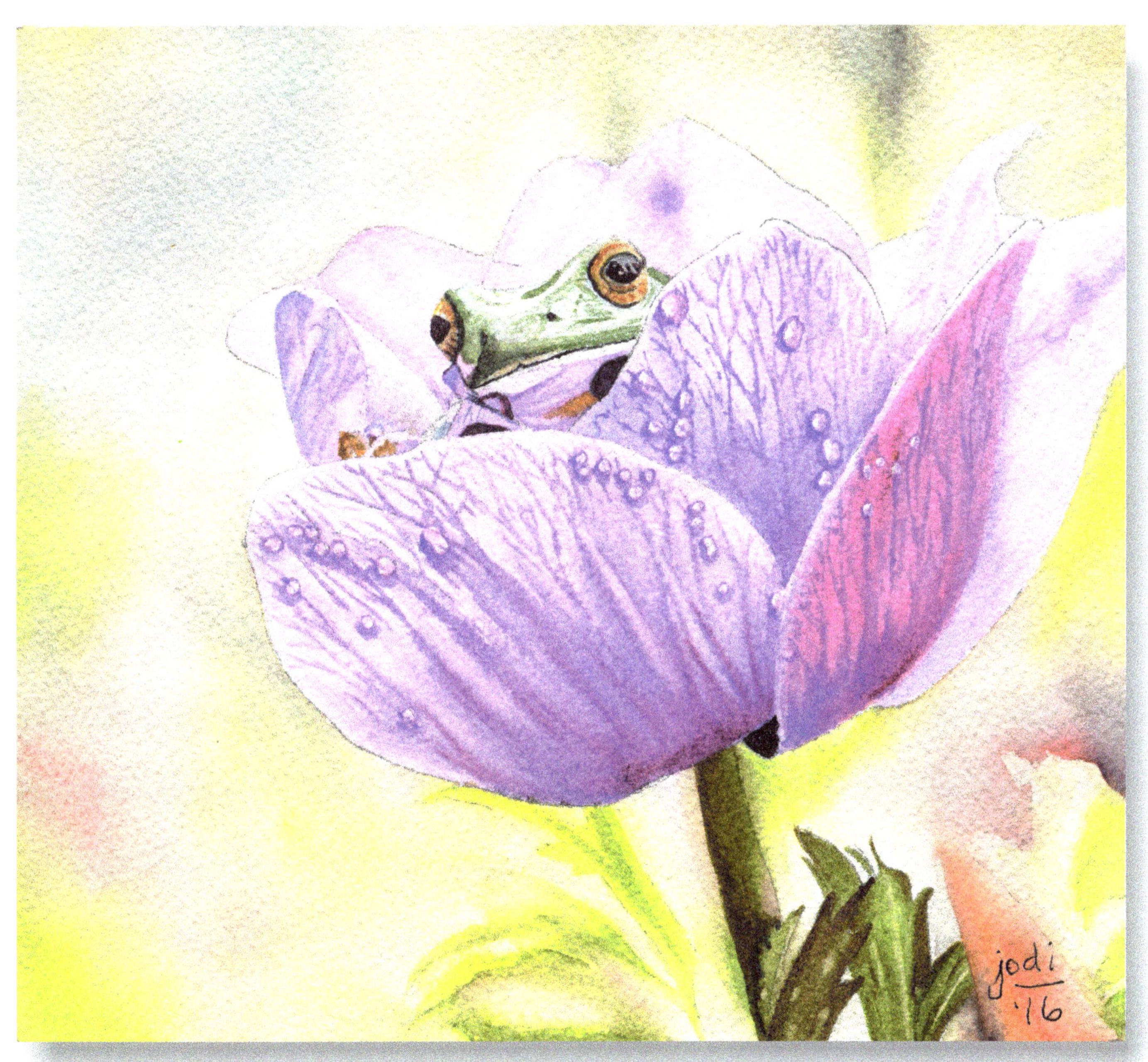
jodi
'16

Wet Pussy Willow

This is the first time I tried water drops, and it would have to be on a furry Pussy Willow bud. More fur fun.

Reference image from Puzzles For Friends
4 7/8" by 6 3/4" on Strathmore 140 pound cold press watercolor paper

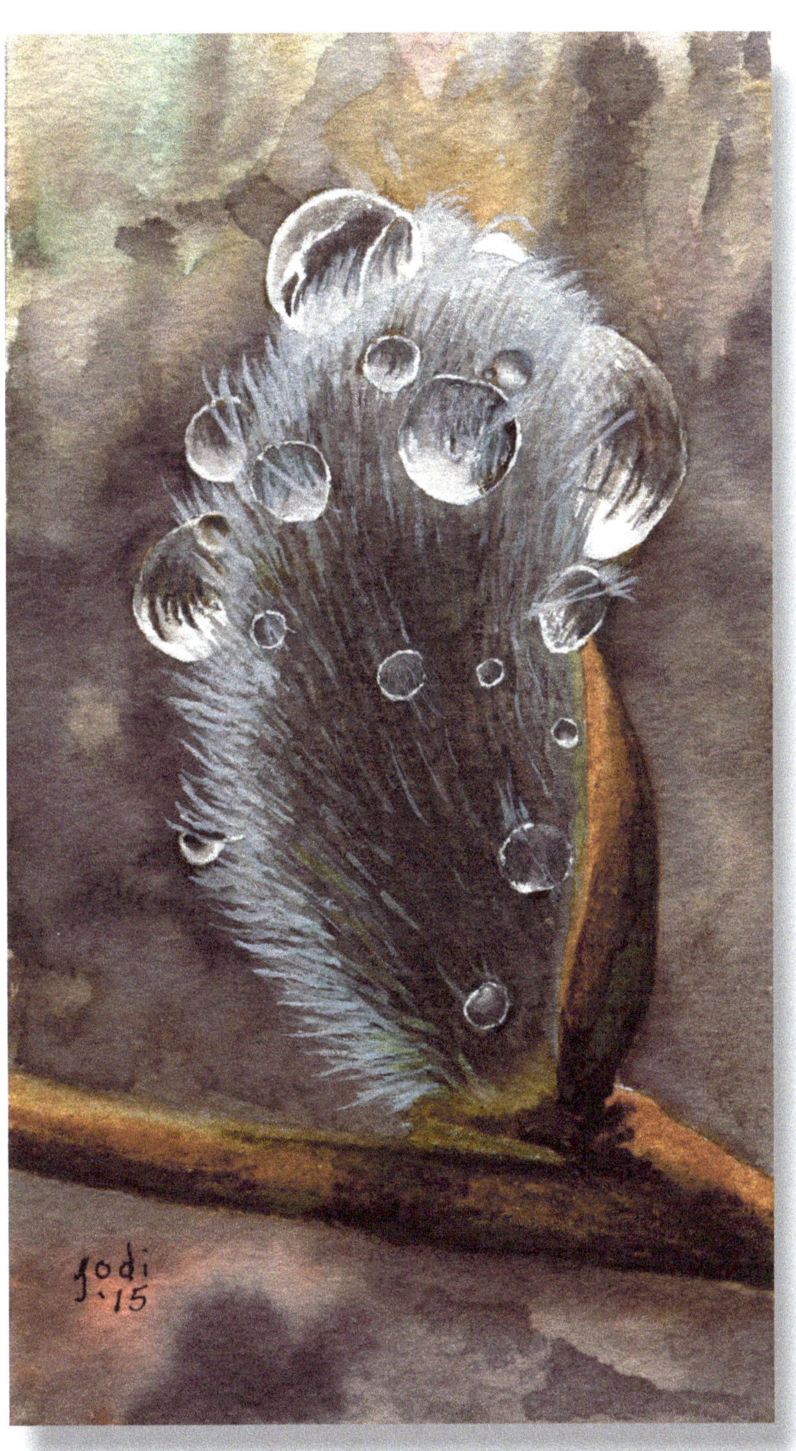
Jodi
'15

TEACH Services, Inc.
PUBLISHING

www.ingramcontent.com/pod-product-compliance
Lightning Source LLC
LaVergne TN
LVHW070919120826
845154LV00019BB/26

* 9 7 8 1 4 7 9 6 1 0 1 9 8 *